Music Scoring for TV
& Motion Pictures

No.779
$12.95

Music Scoring for TV & Motion Pictures
By Marlin Skiles

TAB BOOKS
Blue Ridge Summit, Pa. 17214

ABOUT THE AUTHOR

Marlin Skiles, composer and arranger of more than 135 film scores, is one of those gifted composer/conductors who has been able to keep pace with a rapidly advancing and continuously changing industry. His early career found him as a pianist and arranger with such leading jazz bands as Russ Columbo, Paul Whiteman, and Ben Bernie. He was later able to keep abreast of trends and technology by moving from radio to television and then to film and theater.

His career has led him to be associated with all the major film, radio, and television studios. Yet, he found time to sit on the Board of Directors for San Diego's Opera Guild. With his career came the opportunities for worldwide travel, enabling him to observe and appreciate styles and trends of music throughout the world. He has written original scores for television and film in Mexico City, Rome, Munich, Brussels, and Copenhagen.

Skiles began his career studying piano and theory at the noted Froehlich Conservatory in Harrisburg, Pennsylvania. Later interests brought him to Hollywood, where he studied composition with Dr. Ernst Toch, and conducting with Albert Coates.

FOR ELLA

Contents

Preface

A wide gap in communication has always existed between the functions of *producer/director* and *film composer* for the simple reason that those responsible for production have no common point of reference with those who are to create a musical score. This does not mean that a course in theory, harmony, and counterpoint should be necessarily undertaken by a producer/director. Nor does it imply that film entertainment has suffered drastically because of this verbal gap. Rather, it is my contention that a very real and noticeable artistic improvement could be achieved if this gap could be bridged. One objective of this book is to provide the foundation for that bridge.

It is, of course, an unfortunate fact that many—indeed, most—producer/directors are unable to hear, read, or otherwise audit the music to be supplied by the composer until a physical recording of this music is made. The motion picture as an art form would certainly be better served if this were not so. Why? The reasons are pretty elementary when you consider a few facts.

First, we must acknowledge that the producer can't monitor the progress of a film's musical compositions until the composer has invested a substantial amount of time in preparation of the score. Is it any wonder, then, that he avoids the risks of innovation? Or that he commissions established professionals to provide formula works that have proved themselves in countless earlier motion pictures?

Second, we must understand that the producer/director is operating within a specific budget of both time and money—which all too often means that his efforts will be affected at least to some degree by commercialism. In this book, I contend that commercialism may be preserved without compromising the art form that music and imagery represent. In other words, an artist's creativity need not be unduly restrained or tethered so long as he has some specific direction in mind at the outset. While no book can offer this variable as an entity in itself, I try here to provide enough useful general information to simplify the orientation process for today's film and television composers.

But there is yet another facet of scoring to consider, the most important of them all—the audience. It is unfortunate but true that an individual's appetite for the emotional stimulus that music unquestioningly adds to the film is either satiated or dulled by the constant bombardment of his ears by music in his everyday life: jukeboxes, in-the-office background music, home stereo, auto radios and tape players—they have an appalling tendency to render him virtually numb to the nuances and subtleties of an otherwise truly effective musical score.

Leonard Bernstein, in his book, *The Infinite Variety of Music*, describes it most clearly:

> "... for one thing, we hear too much music... I didn't say we *listen* too much; I said we *hear* too much. There's a big difference between listening—which is an active experience, participating in the music, riding with it up and down and in and out of its involvements and evolvements—and just hearing, which is completely passive. That's what we've got too much of—the eternal radio and TV set, this cursed Muzak, plaguing us from coast to coast, in jets and trains and depots and restaurants and elevators and barbershops. We get music from all sides, music we *can't* listen to, only hear. It becomes a national addiction; and music therefore becomes too undifferentiated. We reach a saturation point; our concentration is diminished, our ears are too tired for real listening...."

The all too common answer is to replace nuances with dissonance or volume or magnitude—like driving a tack with a sledgehammer. The effectiveness of this approach is lost, of course, when the job *really* calls for a sledgehammer.

Film music—*all* of it—exists for a purpose: to add that dimension which cannot be achieved with visuals, dialog, or special effects.

In television production, music, an abstract art form, suffers painfully in the creative process. A 30-minute TV series, exhibited once a week, demands a production time schedule that is so compact that it is startling. This pressure is not felt quite as much in preproduction and shooting as in the final phase—the music contribution. Any delays, which are quite common prior to this period, are felt as a backlash by the composer, who will be faced with time allotted (usually much too short to begin with) cut by 30% or even 50% of the original commitment. It is therefore inconceivable that much deep creative thought can be considered—hence, the similarity and sterility of a great amount of music applied to TV.

True, more than one composer can be and many times *is* commissioned for a single program; but this serves to defeat the theory of *cohesion* or form in the overall music plan for the individual program.

There seems to be no universal solution to this dilemma so long as TV programs are geared to mass production much like the production lines at General Motors and Ford. But there are avenues the composer can take to minimize the untoward effects. This book explores some of these.

Marlin Skiles

The Mechanics
of Scoring

To communicate a musical directive, a necessary first step is the understanding of the various words, abbreviations, and symbols used in the graphic presentation of music. Without these, music could be likened to literature without punctuation. With the exception of isolated German, French, American, or English composers who at times will use their native language, dynamics (Table 1-1) are written in Italian.

The next step is understanding tempo and expression marks, some of the latter of which are included in the listing of dynamics.

The clockwork metronome, invented around the turn of the nineteenth century by Johann Nepomuk Maelzel, has been the basis for tempo of all Occidental music. The normal professional orchestral score will, at the beginning, note the tempo in two ways—a letter/number combination designating the Maelzel metronome beats per minute (such as *MM 120*), and the Italian tempo indication (such as *allegretto*). The quarter note preceding the metronome designation at the top of Fig. 1-1 means that each quarter note will receive one beat at the 120-beat-per-minute rate.

Metronomic indications will vary from very slow, *MM 40*, to very fast, *MM 208*. The higher the numerals, the greater the speed. Since film scores usually specify tempo, film

Table 1-1. Music Dynamics (Terms, Symbols, Meaning).

NOMENCLATURE	SYMBOL OR ABBREV.	MEANING
ACCELERANDO	*accel*	GRADUALLY IN-CREASING THE SPEED
ADAGIO	*adg° or ad°*	SLOWLY, LEISURELY
AD LIBITUM	*ad lib*	AT THE PLEASURE OF THE PERFORMER-IMPROVIZATION
AFFETTO (AFFETTUOSO)	*affett*	EMOTION, TENDER-NESS, PASSION
AGITATO	*ag° or agit°*	EXCITED, AGITATED
ALLA BREVE	¢	A 4/4 BAR WITH ONLY 2 BEATS (FIRST & THIRD)
ALLARGANDO		SAME AS LARGANDO
ALLEGRETTO	*alltt°*	WITH MODERATE SPEED, LIVELY
ALLEGRO	*all°*	RAPIDLY, LIVELY
ANDANTE	*and'ᵉ*	MODERATELY SLOW
ANIMATO	*anim°*	LIVELY, SPIRITED, WITH ANIMATION
APPASSIONATO	*appas*	WITH EMOTION, PASSION
ARCO		IN STRING INSTRU-MENTS, TO BE PLAYED WITH THE BOW
ASSAI		VERY; AS IN **ALLE-GRO** ASSAI - VERY RAPID
BRILLANTE	*brill*	SPARKLING, SHOWY, BRILLIANT
BRIO		SPIRIT, VIVACIOUSNESS
CALANDO	*cal*	DECREASING IN LOUD-NESS AND TEMPO
A CAPPELLA		SINGING WITHOUT INSTRUMENTAL ACCOMPANIMENT
CAPRICCIO		CAPRICIOUS, SIMILAR TO **SCHERO**
CODA		THE FINISH OF A MOVEMENT OR AN ENDING FOR A REPETI-TION OF THE FIRST SUBJECT
COME		AS, LIKE
COMMODO		WITH EASE, LEISURELY
CON		WITH
CRESCENDO	*cresc*	INCREASING IN VOLUME
DA CAPO	*d c*	AT THE BEGINNING
DECRESCENDO	*decresc*	DECREASING IN VOLUME

Table 1-1 continued

NOMENCLATURE	SYMBOL OR ABBREV.	MEANING
DIMIMUENDO DIMINUENDO	*dim*	SAME AS **DECRES-CENDO**
DIVISI	*div*	A SERIES OF TWO OR MORE NOTES ON THE STAFF TO BE PLAYED DIVIDED
DOLCE	*dol*	SWEET, SOFTLY
ELEGANTE		ELEGANTLY, GRACEFUL
ENERGICO		VIGOROUS, ENERGETIC
EROICO (EROICA)		STRONG, HEROIC
ESPRESSIONE, CON	*espress*	WITH EXPRESSION
FERMATA	⌒	A HELD NOTE OR CHORD
FEROCE		FIERCE, WILD, VEHEMENT
FINE		FINISH, CLOSE, END
FORTE	*f*	LOUD, STRONG
FORTEPIANO	*fp*	HEAVY ACCENT FOLLOWED IMMEDIATE-ELY BY SOFT, SUS-TAINED
FORTISSIMO	*ff or fff*	VERY OR EXTREMELY LOUD
FORZA	*forz*	VIGOROUS
FORZANDO		STRONG ACCENT
FUOCO		WITH FIRE, SPIRITED
FURIOSO (FURIOSA)		PASSIONATE, FURIOUS
GIOCOSO (GIOCOSA)		HUMOROUS, PLAYFUL
GIUSTO (GIUSTA)		STRICT, EXACT, AS TEMPO GUISTO - EXACT TEMPO
GLISSANDO	*gliss*	SLIDING FROM ONE NOTE TO ANOTHER
GRAN PAUSA	*g p*	LONG PAUSE
GRANDIOSO	*grand*	MAJESTIC, IN A GRAND MANNER
GRAVE		HEAVY, SLOWLY, SERIOUS, GRAVE
GRAZIOSO	*graz*	ELEGANT, GRACEFULLY
LAGRIMANDO		PLAINTIVE, COMPLAINING
LAGRIMOSO		TEARFUL, LAMENTING
LAMENTANDO (LAMENTOSO)		SAD, MELANCHOLY
LANGUENDO (LANGUENTE)		PLAINTIVE

Table 1-1 continued

NOMENCLATURE	SYMBOL OR ABBREV.	MEANING
LARGAMENTE		BROADLY, WITHOUT CHANGE OF TEMPO
LARGANDO		SLOWER, MARKED WITH POSSIBLE CRESCENDO
LARGO (SUPERL. LARGHISSIMO		SLOWEST TEMPO MARK: BROADLY
LEGATO (SUPERL. LEGATISSIMO)		SMOOTHLY, CONNECTED, UNBROKEN
LEGGIERAMENTE LEGGIERO	*leg*	LIGHTLY, SWIFTLY
LEGNO, COL		TO BE PLAYED WITH THE STICK OF THE BOW (STRINGS)
LENTO		SLOWLY, BETWEEN ADANTE AND LARGO
LOCO		TO BE PLAYED AS WRITTEN; USUALLY FOLLOWS PASSAGE MARKED 8 vs (ONE OCTAVE HIGHER)
L'ISTESSO		THE SAME TEMPO
LUNGA		LONG PAUSE
MAESTOSO	*maest°*	MAJESTIC, DIGNIFIED
MARCATO	*marc*	DISTINCT, MARKED EMPHASIS
MARZIALE		MARTIAL, WARLIKE
MENO	*men*	SLOWER, USUALLY COUPLED WITH **MOSSO (MENO MOSSO)**
MESTO		SAME AS **LAMENTANDO**
MEZZO		HALF
MISTERIOSO	*mist*	MYSTERIOUS
MODERATO	*mod^{t»}*	MODERATE TEMPO
MOLTO		VERY, MUCH, AS **MOLTO ALLEGRO-** VERY FAST
MORENDO	*mor*	DYING AWAY, GROWING SOFTER AND SLOWER
MOSSO		RAPID, AS **MENO MOSSO** (LESS RAPID) OR **PIU MOSSO** (MORE RAPID)
MOTO		MOVEMENT (**CON MOTO**: WITH MOVEMENT)
PESANTE		FIRM, HEAVY
PIACERE		SAME AS **AD LIBITIM**
PIANO PIANISSIMO	*p-pp-ppp*	SOFTLY, VERY SOFT EXTREMELY SOFT

Table 1-1 continued

NOMENCLATURE	SYMBOL OR ABBREV.	MEANING
PIU		MORE (**PIU MOSSO:** MORE SPEED)
PIZZICATO	*pizz*	PLUCK STRINGS
POCO		A LITTLE
PORTAMENTO	*port*	SAME AS **GLISSANDO**
POSSIBLE		AS POSSIBLE
PRESTO		RAPID, FASTER THAN **ALLEGRO**
PRIMO (PRIMA)		FIRST
PUNTA		POINT OF THE BOW
QUASI		LIKE, SIMILAR
RALLENTANDO	*rall*	SAME AS **RITARDANDO**
RAPIDO		RAPIDLY
RITARDANDO	*rit*	SLOWING THE SPEED
ROBUSTO		BOLD, FIRM
RUBATO		NOT IN STRICT TEMPO; TO BE PLAYED WITH FREEDOM OF EXPRESSION
SCHERZO	*scherz*	LIGHT, HUMOROUS
SECCO	*sec*	DRY
SEGNO, dal	*d s* 𝄋	TO REPEAT FROM THE SIGN
SEGUE	*seg*	CONTINUE TO FOLLOWING
SEMPLICE		PLAIN, SIMPLE
SEMPRE	*sem. or semp*	ALWAYS, CONTINUALLY; (**SEMPRE PIANO:** ALWAYS SOFTLY)
SENZA		WITHOUT (**SENZA SORD:** WITHOUT MUTE)
SFORZANDO	*sfz. sf* (♪)	LOUD ACCENT
SLUR		SAME AS **LEGATO**
SOPRA		SEE COME
SORDINO	*sord*	MUTE
SOSTENUTO	*sost*	SUSTAINED, LIKE **TENUTO**
SPIRITO, con	*spir*	SPIRITED, ENERGETIC
STACCATO	*stacc*	DETACHED, SEPARATED
STINGUENDO		DYING AWAY
STRINGENDO	*string*	SUDDEN ACCELERATION, USUALLY WITH **CRESCENDO**
SUAVE		SAME AS **DOLCE**
SUBITO		SUDDENLY, ABRUPTLY

Table 1-1 continued

NOMENCLATURE	SYMBOL OR ABBREV.	MEANING
TENUTO	ten	EACH NOTE HELD FOR ITS FULL TIME VALUE
TREMOLO	trem	FAST MOVEMENT OF BOW ON STRING INSTRUMENTS OF EACH NOTE; ALSO ROLL ON TYMPANI
TRILL	tr	RAPID MOVEMENT BETWEEN TWO NOTES, USUALLY ONE OR ONE-HALF STEP HIGHER THAN BASIC NOTE
TRISTEZZA (TRISTO - TRISTA)	triste	SAD, MELANCHOLY
TROPPO		RAPID BUT NOT TOO MUCH, AS IN ALLEGRO MA NON TROPPO
TUTTI		ENTIRE GROUP
UNISON	unis	A GROUP OF INSTRUMENTS PLAYING THE SAME NOTE
VELOCE		RAPID, SWIFT
VIBRANTE		VIBRANT, AGITATED TONE
VIBRATO	vib	WAVERING OR TREMULOUS TONE OR EFFECT
VIVACE	viv	SPIRITED, BRIGHT
VOLANTE		LIGHT, SWIFT

composers generally ignore metronomic indications if they will be conducting their own music.

Throughout the music sequence changes of tempo may occur, all of which will have to be indicated in tempo markings. For example, if we have an original tempo of three seconds per bar, which would probably have the direction of ANDANTE (*MM 76*), and further on a faster tempo would be employed, the tempo indication would be PIU MOSSO. Sometimes this is shortened to MOSSO, which is understood to mean *more rapidly*. If, still further on, the tempo would slacken, the tempo mark should read MENO MOSSO. The word *meno* precludes any misunderstanding between the shortened MOSSO and the slower MENO MOSSO. (This latter designation could possibly also be abbreviated to simply MENO.) Consequently, the word MOSSO would indicate more rapidity and MENO would indicate less speed.

The score page would appear as shown in Fig. 1-1. And so throughout the sequence, tempo directions are given not only

Fig. 1-1. Tempo directives, timing indications on score sheet.

for the benefit of the conductor but for the musicians who will be performing the music.

The three basic clefs (treble, bass, and viola or *alto*) that appear in the score are shown in Fig. 1-2.

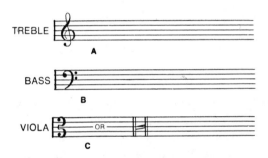

Fig. 1-2. The basic clefs: (A) treble, (B) bass, and (C) viola or alto.

Timing is indicated by stacked numerals adjacent to the clefs. In the top staff of Fig. 1-3. The upper 4 means four beats. The lower 4 means quarter notes.

The next step is to observe passages in the music that are either marked SOLO or SOLI. The former means any single instrument in the orchestra that will perform important sections that are intended to stand out. The plural SOLI indicates that the passage will be played by more than one instrument. In the violin section the word SOLO would therefore designate that only one violin would perform the passage. The directive would usually be the PRIMO symbol I^o (SOLO I^o means first violin). If SOLI were written it would mean that the entire

Fig. 1-3. Stacked numerals on staves indicate number of fractional notes per bar.

section would play the passage. When a specific number of musicians are designated, an uppercase letter A is accompanied by a superscript indicating that number (SOLI A^2, SOLI A^3, etc.).

By being aware of these markings one can very quickly sense the passages in the music that are of prime importance.

The word SOLI does not necessarily mean that passages will only be played in unison (all playing the same notes in the same register) or that the section will be played by only one group of instruments. It can be applied to any combination of instruments in any register such as flute and bassoon; flute, bassoon, and horn; clarinet and viola; oboe and clarinet; etc.

The symbol 8va in the uppermost staff of Fig. 1-4 indicates that the passage is to be played one octave higher. 16va would mean two octaves higher. When the passage is to be played one or two octabes lower, the indication would be 8va BASSA or 16va BASSA. The term LOCO directs this player to perform this music in the written register.

The more common music writing abbreviations are depicted in Fig. 1-4.

WEIGHT

Our next examination is sound volume or *weight*. The heaviest weight in the orchestra is in the brass and percussion sections. Under certain circumstances, the piano and organ

Fig. 1-4. Music staves with directional symbols.

can also give a considerable amount of strength. Weight can be achieved, to a degree, in the string section and of lesser intensity in the woodwind section.

The degrees of weight are governed by the dynamic instructions to the players. The range runs from *ppp* (very soft) to *fff* (very loud) but even *ppp* played by the brass group, percussionists (drums and tympani), piano, or organ will still add weight. In scanning a music score, this must be taken into consideration, particularly when the music is to accompany dialog. If a scene includes low, sparse dialog, it would indeed be unwise to have the distracting effect of the brass group performing in any but its lowest or softest volume. This would also apply to percussion and piano. (The use of these instruments, even in the most polite form, must be very carefully and judiciously handled.)

Weight is also achieved in rapidly moving passages in the woodwind and string section; in fact, intensity will be generated in any group of the orchestra, because proper execution of rapidly moving passages will necessitate a more intense approach.

Tempo of the music is of equal importance. A rapid tempo in music will always create the illusion of increasing the speed of the dramatic action, whether it be dialog, static photography, fights, walking, riding, or whatever. Slow flowing music will create the illusion of decreasing the dramatic tempo.

With this in mind the composer must first assess the feeling of the scene's tempo and then make the decision as to which music speed will best assist the progress of the filmed sequence—to make it move, slow down, or be in direct relation to the dramatic tempo. The mere *application* of music will give an entirely different pulsation to film sequences, as against viewing them without music.

COLOR

Tone color can be defined as the various sounds individual instruments or combinations of instruments display within their respective ranges or registers. The basic color in all instruments can be modified or altered by the players in accordance with the written dynamics. The double-reed instruments—oboe, English horn, and bassoon—are the least flexible because of their individualistic tones. Their sharpness and penetration make them not too compatible in group playing with other instruments. An exception could be the bassoon playing in the high register, whose softer tone makes it possible to blend better with some other instruments such as the French horns.

SKETCH AND SCORE EXAMPLES

In the music sketch depicted in Fig. 1-5, there is no metronome indication; rather, the cumulative duration of each bar, in seconds, is given. A further directive, as to the tempo, is ANDANTE (moderately slow), with a further directive, SEMPRE LEGATO (always smooth flowing). Our next observation should be the $^4/_4$ marking, meaning four quarter notes per bar, with the letter p (PIANO) between the staves.

All of this communicates to the musician that this section of the music will be played softly, constantly smooth flowing, and will move at a fairly slow speed.

Fig. 1-5. Composer's sketch with timing indications.

An orchestrated score of the drafted sketch is shown in Fig. 1-6. Here, additional performance directions have been added.

Fig. 1-6. Opening bars of orchestrated sketch (from Fig. 1-5), showing slurs.

These arcs are called *slurs*; their function is to advise the musician that the passage is to be played smoothly and unbroken (LEGATO).

In the orchestrated score of Fig. 1-7, the composer has elected to write the passage in the first and second bars for the first clarinet SOLI. This means that he will be playing the music with another instrument; scanning down the page will show that the vibraphone is to play the passage with the clarinet. The violins are marked DIV (divided). There are eight violins, two of which will be playing each note. The word TUTTI is

23

Fig. 1-7. Orchestrated score with instrument directives.

written at the third bar (violins). This is a directive that all four violins in this half of the section will play the same notes. The term UNISON could also be used.

Fig. 1-8. Continuation of music sketch, with instrumentation, note tempo change in bar 8.

Figure 1-8 is a continuation of the sketch (of Fig. 1-5), with the first indication of instrumentation: two flutes in the fifth bar. A change of tempo appears in bar eight, meaning that the count in seconds will have to be compensated for in this bar.

24

Each previous bar consumed 3 seconds, but a shorter count is required in bar eight since it contains only three beats.

In Fig. 1-9, which is a continuation of the score, the two flutes are written SOLI A^2, meaning that both will be playing the same notes in unison. They continue through the eighth bar with only the string group as accompaniment. The addition of the vibraphone at the end of the seventh bar serves only to give an added color to the flutes with the symbol of *p* indicating that the passage is of lesser importance.

Fig. 1-9. Orchestrated version of sketch bars 5, 6, 7, and 8.

In the continuation of the sketch (Fig. 1-10) compensation is shown in seconds for the shorter three beat bars. Only 2 seconds are allotted for each $^3/_4$ bar, whereas 3 seconds were used for the previous $^4/_4$ bars.

In the ninth and tenth bars we see more notes to be played than have appeared before. Although the tempo remains

Fig. 1-10. Bars 9 through 12 of music sketch.

constant, this will produce more movement in the music with a slight increase in intensity. In the eleventh bar the conductor is allowed a RITARDANDO (decreasing the speed) with which he can meet the 30-second point at the beginning of bar twelve. The indication here is a return to the tempo of the beginning of the music (TEMPO I⁰).

The orchestration of sketch bars 9−12 (Fig. 1-11) shows that more weight has been given to bars 9 and 10, the two clarinets playing SOLI with the two violas. Up to this point only one or two instruments have been playing the leading passages; this use of four instruments playing the same notes will give added weight. COLLA I° (second clarinet part) is a directive to the copyist to copy the notes of the first (PRIMO) clarinet part.

In the twelfth bar the analysis becomes quite clear. The oboe will be playing the important phrase with the clarinets and the entire string group directed to play MEZZO PIANO (*mp*). A certain amount of weight will be encountered here in the

Fig. 1-11. Orchestrated version of sketch bars 9, 10, 11, and 12.

writing for the clarinets and strings, but it should not create an imbalance because of the assertive quality of the oboe.

In the 13th to 16th bars (Fig. 1-12) a sense of movement is indicated (because of the many notes written in bars 13 and 15). Time compensation is again exhibited in bar 14, with only two beats in the bar. Simple arithmetic resolves this. Bar 13 is allowed 3 seconds for four beats; consequently, bar 14, with only two beats, would be given half of 3 seconds, or 1½ seconds.

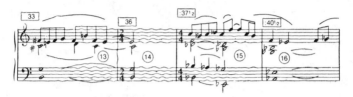

Fig. 1-12. Bars 13 through 16 of music sketch.

In bar 13 of the orchestrated score (Fig. 1-13) we once again find SOLI in the upper violin line. This instructs half the violin section that the phrase is to be executed with more importance. In the 15th bar the flutes continue the phrase (SOLI-UNISON).

The term SOLI has further importance in that the musicians, while performing sections so marked, will instinctively listen to and phrase with any other instrument that will be playing the same passage.

Examine the 4-page score of Fig. 1-14. In the first bar (sheet A), considerable weight is to be expected. The string section, comprising 20 musicians, will be playing FORTE and TREMOLANDO, and the result is a strong intensity. In the second bar, the low strings are fortified by a low trombone, bass clarinet, and piano, with all notes being accented to produce a strong dramatic sound. The first important phrase (third bar) is played by horns and bassoon SOLI. This indicates prime dramatic importance.

In the fourth bar the tension continues, with the strings playing many notes TREMOLANDO. The entrance of the tympani (**mf**—SOLO) in the fifth bar, followed by flutes and clarinets (SOLI) gives another phrase of importance. Bars 7 and 8 (sheet B), with the entire string and woodwind sections marked

Fig. 1-13. Orchestrated version of sketch bars 13, 14, 15, and 16.

TENUTO, will give a very broad dramatic effect. The ninth bar (sheet C) indicates a crescendo leading to the balance of music played FORTE. In the tenth bar, the tympani will be playing SOLO, and this continues to the finish. In bar 11, two clarinets play SOLI with the first clarinet continuing SOLO in the twelfth bar.

In bars 13 and 14 (sheet D) the piano will be playing only three notes, each one, however, SOLO. ACCENTED. and FORTE. The oboe plays two short SOLO passages in the two final bars.

The music is heavily dramatic, not adequate to accompany dialog.

Fig. 1-14 (sheet A). Example of orchestrated music score for analysis.

Fig. 1-14 (sheet B). Example of orchestrated music score for analysis.

Fig. 1-14 (sheet C). Example of orchestrated music score for analysis.

Fig. 1-14 (sheet D). Example of orchestrated music score for analysis.

EXPRESSION DESIGNATIONS IN FILM SCORES

Some film composers are negligent in applying dynamic indications and expression marks to their scores. This neglect usually occurs when the composer intends to conduct his own music and will depend upon verbal instructions to the orchestra. Such music writers are in the minority, however. The foremost film composers are meticulous, and take great pride in leaving no doubt as to how they wish their music to be performed.

The Functional
Elements of Scoring

The present-day film music director is, in the majority of cases, the composite composer/conductor. This hybrid individual is basically a composer who has elected to combine the talents of composing and conducting and be the deciding factor in the performance of his music. This dual faculty has been quite successful in the application of music to films. A probable reason for this is the mechanics involved in the process—music written specifically to timing does not allow a great deal of individual interpretation or freedom of expression. Another contributing factor is the time element, which many times will not allow the necessary interval for a separate conductor to familiarize himself adequately with the score.

This would apply particularly in the present vogue of using a great amount of mixed colors (various combinations of different instrumental sounds) in the writing of film music. A "separate" conductor would need a considerable amount of time to digest all of these sometimes vague tonal combinations in order to perform them satisfactorily.

In symphonic music the talents of the composer and the conductor (music director) are usually widely separated. The conductor has spent many years of study perfecting his talent (as has the composer in developing his); rarely do we find a genuinely successful combination of the two. The genius of a Wagner, Liszt, Mahler, Bernstein, and a few others are the exception. This is not the case when it comes to film music.

The Screen Directors' Guild many years ago won a court decision which denied the use of the term *music director* on screen credits. This ruling was based on the fact that the Guild had an existing contract with a producers' association barring the use of·the term *director* on screen credits to any except the film director.

Up to the time of Guild decision, each major film studio had established the position of *general music director*. This person supervised all music production and at times would conduct other composer's scores or compose and conduct his own music for certain films. Men such as Alfred Newman (20th Century Fox), John Green (Metro-Goldwyn-Mayer), Ray Heindorf (Warner Brothers), and Morris Stoloff (Columbia Pictures) served as directors who worked with teams consisting of composers, orchestrators, arrangers, copyists, music editors, the music contractor (who employed the musicians), and music supervisors.

Today the general music director has disappeared. Independent producers have taken over most of production and have been engaging free-lance composer/conductors on a one-assignment basis for many years. The few Hollywood studios that still maintain a music department usually have as their head, or supervisor, a person that is more of a business executive than a participating musician.

THE COMPOSER/CONDUCTOR

The composer/conductor's responsibilities include suggesting the basic music plan for the production—that is, a general overall approach to the mood or feeling of the anticipated music. This is formulated during conferences with the producer/director before, during, or after viewing the edited version of the production. At this time, decisions are made pertaining to which sequences will be accompanied by music, which will be prerecorded, as well as the sizes and types of orchestra that will perform the music.

In dramatic productions he may be requested by the producer to submit various thematic ideas—one of which will presumably be chosen by the producer as the foundation or main theme to be used as the basis for the musical score.

Perhaps the most common complaint among composer/conductors is that all too often they are not included in consultations at the beginning phases of constructing the screenplay. They feel that their contribution could be of much greater benefit if they were allowed to become a part of the creative team from the inception of the dramatic production. This lack of early participation, they feel, creates certain handicaps that serve to "box them in," thus damping their obvious creative talents.

The composer's* contribution to a film production has been of increasing importance. With the great advances in recording techniques, the multitude of new electronic and percussion instruments, and the variety of sophisticated instrumental amplification systems at his command, the composer has found many new tools with which to work. The scope of his creative talent has widened to an extent far beyond the imagination of earlier film composers.

His contribution, basically, is to supply music that will assist in plot motivation, heighten dramatic suspense, and convey certain "shock" elements. He uses music as a tool to accomplish specific objectives of a secondary nature—to set a tempo, to bridge from one time period or place to another, to herald a change in dramatic emotion. The composer must be able to convey, through music, a wide array of abstract "thoughts" and the emotions of the actors in order to assure the audience of the actor's thinking or deliberation—and all this must be achieved while providing the musical background necessary to enhance the story or scenic portrayal. In general, music's contribution to the photography is the added complementary emotional stimulus necessary for the full enjoyment of (or involvement in) the plot development.

The composer, in addressing the multifaceted role of his contribution, is faced with many problems and decisions. A delicate thin line separates the music *assistance* from the music *insistence*. The understanding and observation of this

---

*The term composer will be used henceforth, as an abbreviation for composer/conductor except in cases where the function is divided between two people.

division is of utmost importance if he is to achieve the correct balance of music sound and dramatic presentation. His temptation to use the orchestra to its utmost proficiency will be very great. The successful composer learns to temper this urge (remember the sledgehammer).

The decision as to where to employ music and where not to becomes an item of concern for both the composer and the producer.* Much foresight is necessary in this planning: visualization of the final composite result; audience reactions; whether the addition of music will assist or detract from the intention of the scene; weights, colors, and tempo of the music. All of these aspects must be taken into consideration.

Robert Nathan, author of over 40 novels including *Portrait of Jenny* and *The Bishop's Wife*, gave a most simple, direct, and succinct statement regarding this subject: "In discussing the application of music to any given scene, the producer and composer should first ask themselves *why*. Why music here? Why music there?" He goes on further to say:

> "A really good script should not have too much talk in it—too many words. It should have moments of tension and emotion—particularly emotion which you can't put into words. I mean, no matter how good a scriptwriter may be, the fewer words the better, and at that point music should take over to say to the audience what a scriptwriter is not able to say but what a novelist would be able to say by seeing what was going on in the minds of his characters, describing their feelings, by describing the ambience, by describing the landscape—by describing all kinds of things. A novelist has that where a scriptwriter doesn't. A look is not enough. No matter how good the actor, he can't really say everything that he's going through at the moment. Then music is a great help as a bridge. It's an added color, a necessary color that you need there.
>
> A constant flow of music gets in the way. It should not...conflict with dialog...and I don't think it is particularly good for tension. (When it comes to portraying)...insecurity and tension, the less music the better."

It is not necessary to go into lengthy descriptions of the changes that have occurred throughout history in all creative art forms such as painting, sculpture, architecture and music. The cultural revolutions that have caused—or, in some cases, have been caused by—these changes are quite well known.

---

*The term producer is used to indicate either producer/director for the sake of brevity except where these functions are separate.

Music has not been a stepchild in the dramatic upheavals that have occurred over the years.

We find, however, one deviation in these metamorphoses, and that is in film music. Rather than having been responsible for changes within itself, establishing new patterns, progressing by its own initiative through the efforts of its composers to present new ideas, it has generally become a follow-the-leader endeavor.

The early movie-house pianists, because they were not composers, followed the line of least resistance and accompanied films with tired pieces of familiar music. These pieces many times had not the slightest resemblance to the moods of the scenes for which they were supplying the music. During this period opera was at its pinnacle of success. The great masters of opera for years had been successfully describing musically many of the several human emotions; consequently, it would seem only natural to follow along this already charted course instead of using pieces of music such as *Asa's Death*, *The Scarf Dance*, and *William Tell Overture*.

An automobile racing down a road paralleling a speeding railroad train and then crossing a track a split second before the arrival of the train indicated only one thing to these primitive accompanists. Speeding train—speeding automobile: speeding music. A curious fact remains that much of this same technique continues to the present day.

The motivating forces that caused this constant duplication of approach were basically the early producers. These dry goods manufacturers, nickelodeon operators, Tin Pan Alley song pluggers, through their investments in early filmmaking, became the omnipotent authorities in all of the various departments of production—including music. It is understandable, then, that with their music intellects reaching probably no higher than Broadway shows and popular songs they could recognize only approaches that had been heretofore "successful."

Exceptions, however, were occurring. One has only to examine Edmund Meisel's score for *The Battleship Potempkin* to grasp his professional and progressive thinking. The Wagnerian *leitmotif*—a short piece of thematic music or phrase used throughout operas in association with certain characters—probably made its first appearance in music for

American films in the early scores written specifically for certain silent films. In *The Birth of a Nation* the Wagnerian influence not only manifested itself through the use of the leitmotif but also with its heavy handed approach to almost every human emotion. It was tried and true. The use of overabundant music sounds was most successful in silent films because there were no competitive or distractive sound elements—not even dialog or special effects.

With the advent of recorded music for films the Wagnerian influence continued, a contributing reason probably being that what had been successful before *had* to work with carrying the familiar formula into this new infant electronic projection.

It became fashionable for Hollywood to import noted European composers, few of whom had the slightest idea of what this new technique of sound on film was all about. Their basic training in music output had been the symphony, opera, operetta, ballet and the music hall. With men well-grounded in these fields, it is understandable that their film works would include a very narrow approach comparable to their personal classic writings.

Even with Hollywood importing composers, arrangers, and conductors such as Alfred Newman, Leo Forbstein, and Ray Heindorf, the basic Wagnerian patterns had been set. And they were followed as the accepted formula for motion picture scoring: The accelerated, wild ponderous music for chases. Thick, lush sounds for love scenes. Heavy, dark colors for dramatic sequences. Tremolo strings with hesitant celli and contrabasses for mystery. They all overplayed the emotions as specified by the script and the actors.

Then some composer became familiar with the music of Delius. The surprising and unconventional chord progressions of such compositions as *Brigg Fair* and *In a Summer Garden*, struck the fancy of composers as just the *right* music sounds for normal background—discounting chases and fights, of course, which still had to remain Wagnerian because one couldn't have a 70-piece orchestra available and allow any of the personnel to be idle while performing music for such scenes of violence.

On problem arose, however, during the Delius period: any attempt to disguise the basic and subtle chord progressions and melodic lines still came out *pure Delius*. So what next?

Why not investigate the French school and try Debussy, Ravel, and Ibert?

This they did. *Afternoon of a Faun*, *La Mer*, *Nocturnes*, *Daphnis and Chloe*, *Ports of Call*...all were twisted, turned, revised, and paraphrased. In fact, the score for *Portrait of Jenny* contained Dimitri Tiomkin's arrangements of Debussy.

While all this was going on there were a few composers who approached the medium from the standpoint of its being another version of the theater. No classic composer nonsense but purely their own music written in the way they felt best suited the film. Men such as George Antheil, Hans Eisler, Kurt Weill, George Auric, Aaron Copland, and Bernard Herrmann, with their own individual idiomatic expressions, attempted to instill new life into film music. But with the exception of Copland they established no definite trend to be followed. It is difficult to understand why Copland's early American style of music, as exemplified in *Appalachian Spring*, made a lasting impression on some film composers which, unfortunately, many have never been able to cast off.

During the late thirties there was a swing toward Gershwin; but this style, due to its jazz orientation, was limited to lighter film scores. But Hollywood composers slowly established their own individual idioms and moved away from the classic influence. Alfred Newman, Roy Webb, Adolph Deutsch, Max Steiner, Victor Young, Franz Waxman and others of like stature brought film music to its highest level, which so far has not been surpassed—in fact it's had a frightening deterioration, as will be explained.

The billion-dollar phonograph recording industry has had by far the most significant effect on film music. Even with the great influence on classical music by Bach, Haydn, and Mozart; the romantic period of Shumann, Schubert, Brahms; the Russian and French schools—none had as great an impact on creative music as phonograph recordings have had on music for films.

Phonograph recordings of themes from motion pictures are, of course, not new. As early as 1931 we find that Alfred Newman's *Sentimental Rhapsody* from Street Scene was recorded on disc; in 1934 Prokofiev's score for *Lieutenant Kije*; 1935, Max Steiner's *The Informer*; 1936, Virgil

Thompson's *The Plow That Broke The Plains* and Charles Chaplin's *Smile* from Modern Times. Of all of these recordings only two withstood the test of time: Newman's *Sentimental Rhapsody* and Chaplin's *Smile*, the former of which became a light symphonic jazz classic and the latter a popular song that continues to be a standard to this day.

It may have all started with Richard Addinsell's *Warsaw Concerto* from Dangerous Moonlight. The success of this piece of music was a complete accident. At the outset it was not intended to be a phonograph record, but after the release of the film audience requests for the recordings of the music were so numerous that a rejected take for the film sequence was salvaged and rushed into disc release even with its abundance of minor mistakes in the performance. Film producers and phonograph recording executives soon got the message. Even though theme music was used extensively in films since the inception of sound, this incident opened the door for a new and important source of revenue.

In 1944 another excerpt from a film score made history. David Raksin's *Laura*. With the success of *Warsaw Concerto* it would seem only natural that a disc of this very much above average piece of music would have been released immediately. Not so. The same situation existed as with *Dangerous Moonlight*. Score written. Music recorded. And again not until the audience demand for phonograph recordings reached a high level was the disc released.

In 1952, Dimitri Tiomkin's memorable theme from *High Noon* was undoubtedly intended from the outset to be released as a phonograph record. This pattern has continued until the present day.

A large percentage of the cost of producing a phonograph record is exploitation. It is difficult then to understand why much movie music was ignored. After all, this music needed very little wide exposure, thereby decreasing the high cost of phonograph record exploitation considerably.

Eventually, film producers established, bought, or went into partnership with music publishers and phonograph recording companies, and the result was a tidy moneymaking package. This became a dictating influence in much of film music production—particularly so with rock and roll. Here, we had music designed for phonograph records and then applied to films. In essence, the disc trends became the bible for much motion picture music. This was a complete turnaround from the "normal" approach of playing to enhance the dramatic and emotional motivations of the plot.

Renowned composer John Green was asked for his opinion of the current trend in using rock groups to score certain feature films. "This is the kind of question that can make me come off like Carry Nation," he said. "And I'd like to dissect my answer:

> "There is nothing intrinsically anatomic to be condemned in the use of any sound that is an appropriate adjunct to dramatic action—whether it be the explosive crack of a cannon, the slam of a door, or the sound of rock music if it suits the film. My attitude toward the whole syndrome represented by the question is that the barometer has been altered. The proper barometer is, *What is right for the picture from the point of view of its internal dramaturgy?* Instead, the barometer seems to have become, *What will give us a sale of a million phonograph record singles and a quarter million in soundtrack albums?* Therefore, we have a reversal in the order of thinking. We now have a situation in which, instead of evaluating what is correct for the picture—what musical texture, what musical style, what form of musical structure in expression properly enhances the film in the theatre, the impact of the picture on the theatre audience—the producer starts by asking what's great for the phonograph business and, having decided what's great for the phonograph business, he then shoehorns that into his picture.
>
> "We who have served apprenticeships and who have grown up step by step and learned our trade in the scoring of pictures know that, in addition to its esthetic values, it is a highly technical form of expression. I hold in total disdain a group of people—however successful they may be at the *Troubador*, or on the Capitol or A&M label—who haven't the vaguest idea of the difference between a sprocket hole, a flywheel, and a projector lens and to whom Moviola is probably a form of frying oil. I am so incensed by all of this that I cannot really give you a totally valid and unimpassioned answer. At the same time, it is invalid to say categorically that no rock group can produce a great score for a certain kind of motion picture. I realize that this is a labyrinthine answer but there isn't a simpler one."

The same question was asked of Quincy Jones, a prominent film and television composer who himself was formerly a vice-president for Mercury Records:

> "Sometimes it functions very well, but I think the enchantment, the unique quality that a rock group can bring, has to include a person that understands film scoring. I don't understand why it hasn't happened. The results might be particularly rewarding if producers dealt with a group like *Chicago* (they've tried) or *Blood Sweat and Tears*. Both groups have members who have great musical backgrounds, and I think they could turn out a very effective score for the right kind of picture."

Mr. Jones was then asked, *Do you feel that in many cases the decision to use rock groups is based primarily on the hope for a hit record?*

> "Absolutely. they like to associate with success and they like to deal with rock groups that are successful. They usually want to ride with the exploitation value of a hit album. They are very hung up with this 'success by association' now. They discovered it four or five years ago and are all experts now."

Does this not ignore the basic function of music in films: to hence the story? "Sometimes," says Jones,

> "—in fact. most of the time when they are trying to 'squeeze a group in.' they don't really know how to do it. But I think there can be very effective ways of using contemporary music in films."

The influence of phonograph recordings has had a further, most interesting, effect. Some film producers, during the editing period, have had tape copies made of existing phonograph recordings and have used these tapes as temporary music tracks to accompany certain scenes during the cutting or editing process.

In at least two cases, *The Graduate* and *2001—A Space Odyssey*, the producers became so enamored with the feel or music sound accompanying these scenes that the phonograph discs were used as the final music track of the production. Again, Robert Nathan's view:

> "To me it's simply a single chord constantly delivered with certain rhythmical changes. and the lyrics are the utmost in banality. They are very ordinary thoughts expressed in the most ordinary possible way. It serves as poetry when it is not poetry at all. It has little wit—almost no rhyme scheme or meter—it's like saying 'I feel sort of sad today. so I think I'll go home and get some of mother's good cooking.' That serves as a lyric. You can take those words. for instance. and put in an insistent drum beat and thump on the guitar. with two chords (no more than two chords). no melody whatsoever. and have it intoned into a microphone by some half-man. half-woman. sounding as much as possible like a black soprano woman—and all of a sudden you have a rock hit. I think the title music for *The Graduate* is one of the most offensive. rude. and cruel bits of lyric writing I have ever heard. I never could see the slightest excuse for it."
>
> "It is interesting to note that the first rock song was possibly in the Brecht-Weill opera. *Mahagonny*. It was called *Moon of Alabama*. The song was complete nonsense. a complete spoof. The ending line was *I have to have whiskey or I'll die*. which came from out of nowhere at the end of each stanza. This. I think. was father to the rock trend. At least *Somewhere My Love* from 'Doctor Zhivago' is a melody. It's not necessarily Beethoven's *Ninth* but it *is music*."

Might we not conclude that the film and television industry is, in many cases, putting the cart before the horse by excessive commercialization of its music—allowing money to dictate art and culture, contributing very little, if anything, to the progress of music in films? Perhaps. But it would be remiss to discuss film music by certain composers who, by their stature and very mature thinking, have produced scores that are above such adverse criticism. Alex North, Jerry Goldsmith, John Barry, Leonard Rosenman, Hugo Friedhofer, and others in this high echelon of film composing talent have been able to avoid the phonograph recording pressures to a great extent. True, they have not deliberately avoided thematic writing. This is certainly necessary in the application of music to a considerable number of films. But they have been able to handle this delicate situation in a most objective manner. Further, they have been able to combine the attractive popular varied rhythmic structures with advanced approaches in scoring with the normal film orchestras.

The influence in the writing by these people on the progress of film music can only be considered of utmost importance in giving new life to motion picture and television music.

In his approach to a film production the composer should bring expert knowledge of the craftsmanship of music application to the cinema as well as a unique creative talent specifically designed for this form of entertainment.

The mechanics entailed are many. Timing procedures, guide tracks, music cue or timing guide sheets, suitability of the use of metronomic click tracks, and a host of others, all of which will be examined in detail in later chapters, are vitally necessary to achieve a smooth operation.

A thorough knowledge of these mechanics is of utmost importance if from only an economic standpoint. All film production is based on budget with certain sums allotted to the various functions necessary to complete the endeavor. True, there is a degree of flexibility in these planned budgets; but the mechanics of music, which many times is not considered artistic, suffers from a lack of budget flexibility.

Unfortunately, there are few sources of learning for this craft, and it indeed presents a problem for the young composer who has not had the advantage of practical experience.

With acquired technical knowledge, the composer should bring to the production a sense of the theatre—either opera, ballet, dramatic, or musical theatre. An understanding of all of these art forms is most helpful. Along with this, his creative expertise must be extremely flexible since he will be presented with a variety of subject matter in many films he plans to score. No two dramatic sequences will be alike. He will be expected to fashion his music to sometimes subtle and sometimes violent emotional changes. He will also be expected to give cohesion to the entire dramatic production and not wander far afield in his overall approach.

His creative ideas can be communicated verbally only to a limited extent, after which he is on his own, alone, to transmit these ideas through an orchestra of sometimes limited size and usually in limited time.

His mental processes should evaluate the given sequences and, after very careful consideration, he must add any necessary flavor, tone, color, or weight that is needed to justify the addition of music.

He should understand and be familiar with current music styles or trends. If he does not feel capable of personally dispensing any unusual types of music, he should have the wherewithal to call on experts in any given field and intelligently supervise their contributions. Let us examine the role of the composer and the ways in which his work impinges on others throughout the creative process of film scoring.

OVERVIEWING THE CREATIVE PROCESS

The beginning of the creative process is, of course, in the composer's mind either from the time he reads the script or after his first viewing of the edited film. Subconsciously or consciously, he will be mentally formulating music sounds that he feels best suited to the approaching chore of writing the notes on paper. We stress the word chore because that is exactly what it is in most cases. Composers don't generally consider writing film music as a lark (notwithstanding Victor Young, who once told me that he would some day write an entire film score in one day!)

It would be impossible to estimate how much music can be turned out in one day, one week, or one month by the average composer. Alex North says that his output is roughly five minutes per week. Other composers may try to write a minimum of two or three minutes per day. Still others, under pressure, could probably double this amount. In all respects, however, the schedule for creating is a completely individual affair.

The formulating of any prime themes, subthemes, or motifs would normally be the first step, following which the composer will personally view the film for deeper analysis of the dramatic intent.

The amount of time a composer will need to view a film before starting detailed writing varies greatly, depending on the subject matter and complications that he may be presented with. David Grusin says:

> "I would say maybe a half-dozen times if this can be managed. I'm a late writer. I used to think that this was procrastination but now I don't really think this is the answer. I spend a lot of time worrying and thinking and rolling the thoughts around before I write anything down. So, during that time the more that I can see the picture, the better off I am. At the same time, I feel that first impressions are really important."

And Quincy Jones:

> "I have a Moviola downstairs and I believe the most essential thing is to know that film. Every cut, every word of dialog, all lighting, every shot...everything affects you. You are giving it back to the screen. So you have to receive all of those impulses over and over again in the subconscious, so that when you are in the process of writing, the same source of music is guided by the motivation and inspiration, and also the awareness of what you are dealing with."

John Green's answer:

> "How many times do I screen a dramatic film before I start writing the score? Many, *many* times. I don't start actual writing until I can practically recite the dialog and delineate the action without looking at my timing sheets. This went for the very short film on which I was recently working just as it did for *Raintree County* which, as you know, was over three hours long."

Hugo Friedhofer:

> "That is a question that calls for considerable thought. I have scored some pictures where the first viewing gave me an overall picture of the kind of music the picture demanded—where the music should go, give or take 10 seconds either way. There have been other films that I viewed as many as five or six times before making up my mind.

"...There is one type of picture that always creates great problems for the composer. and that is a picture which is shot mainly in one interior set and having innumerable places where you can possibly start the music. But once having started. where do you go out? I recall one film in particular where I sat with my music editor. George Adams. at Twentieth Century Fox for a good week of daily viewing. I'd give him notes and then go home and say. *Huh-uh! That was wrong!* and then go back the next day and run it again. The film was titled *The Outcasts of Poker Flat*. which dealt with rather reprehensible characters holed up in a shack in the high Sierras."

The detailed writing of notes on paper begins, in the majority of cases, with a rough sketch similar to the example shown in the last chapter. But the composer can't draft a meaningful sketch until he knows some salient facts about the production. Where will music be used? How much time is allotted for the major sequences to be scored? In other words, the composer's work must be in sync with the photoplay. So the composer must be familiar with some of the technical aspects of filmmaking.

Breakdown of Music Cues

Technical film work is addressed by reels and footages, and music sequences or *cues* are identified in their proper numerical order. For example, the first piece of music to appear in a film may be identified: *M* (for music), *1* (for first reel), *Part 1* (for first cue), or M1 PART 1. In some cases the word *part* is omitted, so the designation becomes *M1-1*, meaning the same, of course. Throughout the balance of the film all of the music cues will be numbered sequentially—M2-1, M2-2, M3-1, etc.

Where the composer begins work during the film's conceptual stages, the creative process may be highly individualized and nonprocedural. In such a case, the composer has only a story script to work from, so he will not necessarily have a firm idea as to where music will appear, how much time is allotted for each music sequence, and other such important factors, though he *will* be in a position to formulate basic musical structures, themes, and in general get an overview of what messages he will be expected to convey through his ultimate score.

When much of the film shooting has been done, however, and viewing of the filmed sequences is possible, the creative process becomes somewhat procedural. The producer and composer attend *spotting sessions*, where they actually view the available film footage and determine together those sequences to be scored. Here, they decide where music will begin and where it will end, with a *music editor* making notes as to the visual or aural cues that identify these key points in the story.

In his cutting room, the music editor will use his notes to construct an overall typewritten thumbnail description (cue sheet) of all music sequences with correct overall timings. He views a copy of the film on a viewing and editing machine, through which the film is run at standard speed and viewed on a miniature ground-glass screen not unlike a small TV screen. This *Moviola* (Fig. 2-1) is also capable of reproducing a sound track (or multiple tracks) in synchronization with the optical film. It can be reversed, stopped, and run forward or backward at advanced and slow speeds.

Fig. 2-1. The Moviola allows footage to be screened at any speed, and is equipped with precision length and time counters to simplify editing.

The music cue sheet allows the composer to gage his work plan based on the total amount of music to be written.

With the aid of this overall guide, the composer will be able to design his thematic material in its proper placements for a well balanced score. This also puts him in a position to decide the various orchestra personnel sizes that will be needed to carry the various filmed sequences.

Figure 2-2 shows an actual overall cue sheet for the movie, *The Violent Ones,* a straightforward yarn about a Mexican-American sheriff confronted with the rape and murder of a young girl in a New Mexico border town. Note identification of film reels, music cues, and precise timing indications.

```
                    OVERALL MUSIC CUE SHEET

                       Production 1102
    REEL  CUE                                    OVERALL LENGTH

      1    1   Girl's room - radio playing           1:00

           2   Main Title - B.G. various
               shots Sheriff's car at speed          2:18

           3   10-3 fr. click loop. Start after
               Sheriff questions suspect - shoves
               him into car - drives back to town.
               Out on sign "Santa Rita"              131 clicks
                   Cross over to cue 4

           4   Hold on sign - car to sheriff's office -
               Mexicans move to car - out on interior
               office                                :54

      2    1   Start after line "—not Mexico?" on cut
               to angry Mexicans.  Out on dial.  "you
               say get 'em"                          :44 1/3

           2   Start after "—take care of you."
               Sheriff to hospital.  Out on "Manuel"  1:10

      3    1   Start after "—let 'em get you.  Shots
               of prisoners.  Out on dial.           :28

           2   Noose on table.  Out on dial.  "inter-
               esting design"                        :09 1/2

           3   After "It might be too late"
               Exterior shot of crowd, Cut to office
               - prisoner brought in - out on dial.  :22 1/3

               ABBREVIATIONS:  B.G. - Background
                               Dial. - Dialog
                                  10-3 fr. click loop -
                                  Each click spaced 10
                                  frames and 3 sprocket
                                  holes apart
```

Fig. 2-2. Overall music cue sheet (The Violent Ones).

After completion of the overall timings, the music editor will compile individual detailed cue sheets for each music sequence. These cue sheets (see example, Fig. 2-3) will designate all dialog, action, fadeouts, fade-ins, dissolves,

```
                    MUSIC CUE SHEET

                   REEL 8 - PART 3

                    PRODUCTION 1102
Seconds
               Start after Vega's dialogue with Lucas, "I could kill
               you - so don't tempt me". He shoves Lucas
  :00          After shove

  :05½         Cut to C.U. - Vega looking hard at Lucas

  :10          Move to full C.U. of Vega - hold on him

  :24          Cut to shot of moon

  :26 2/3      Start 8 ft. dissolve to morning sky

  :29½         Center of dissolve

  :32          Full in on morning sky

  :34 2/3      Cut to 3 shot - Vega, Lucas, Vorzyck - sleeping

  :40          Vorzyck starts to open his eyes

  :45 1/3      He sits up and looks around

  :49          Reacts to something O.S.

  :51 1/3      Cut to long shot - men on horses

  :55          Back to Vorzyck

  :55 1/3      Dialogue - softly - "Lucas, Vega. Wake up"

  :59 1/3      Yells "Come on you guys--------"

 1:05          End dialogue - Lucas looks off at

 1:05 2/3      Long shot - men on horses

 1:07½         Cut back to group, Lucas, "Huh - Where----"

 1:09 2/3      "Over there"

 1:10          Men on horses start to move.

 1:12 1/3      Cut back to group

 1:12 2/3      "Yeah - let's move"

 1:15 2/3      "Come on - move!" They start off

 1:29          Cut to them walking fast around rocks
```

```
                    Reel 8 - Part 3

                        Page  2

 1:38          Vega stops suddenly and looks off

 1:39          Cut to distant light blinking

 1:43          Cut back to group - watching

 1:44 2/3      They start to move again

 1:55 2/3      Cut to close up of man holding mirror

 2:07½         Cut to another blinking light

 2:11½         Cut to another blinking light

 2:15          Cut to Vega and men climbing higher into mountains

 2:31          Cut to another angle - across rocks - Vega pulling men
               toward camera

 2:45          Hold on C.U. Vega standing - looking off

 2:49 1/3      Cut to 2 men on horses - top of hill

 2:51 1/3      Back to Vega watching

 2:52 1/3      End reel 8 - end cue
```

Fig. 2-3. Individual music cue sheet (The Violent Ones).

changes of locale and time, as well as other information that the composer will need for detailed construction of the music score.

All of this will be done with the aid of the Moviola and its footage counter, which will be set at zero at the beginning of each cue, thus giving the running footage through to the end of the sequence. Stops will be made and the footage noted for all inner timings of dialog, action, dissolves, etc. These footages *of film* are converted to seconds and split seconds by means of charts that have been designed for that purpose (Fig. 2-4).

Following the receipt of the cue sheets by the composer, which are normally forwarded to him at the end of each working day, the composer begins the task of detailed writing of the music. His most dependent and necessary tool is now the stopwatch. It will be rare indeed, if not impossible, for any reediting of the film to accommodate any music development that he may have in mind. His thinking must be *locked* firmly to the dictates of this stopwatch, and he must architecturally construct his score within this constraint.

Identification of Cues on Film

After the music has been timed, the music editor prepares the film for recording of the music and final dubbing, recording, or mixing—the final blending of sound effects, music, and dialog onto the master soundtrack after the music recording.

In preparing the film, the music editor will number each cue, on the film, with its proper identification. This is normally printed, by hand, on adhesive tape and then applied to the film some distance prior to where the music will start. This is done for identification purposes only. He will then indicate at the point, or frame, where the music is supposed to begin. He usually does this by scribing a diagonal line from the left edge of the film six or seven feet before the music begins, and ending on the right edge of the film at the starting point of the music. Along with this he will punch a round hole in the specific frame where the music is to start. Another method of visually identifying the start of the music involves the use of punched holes rather than a scribed line.

Further guide marks will be employed in the body of the sequence to assist the conductor, during the recording session, to arrive at certain critical points correctly.

SECONDS	35MM FOOTAGE	16MM FOOTAGE	MINUTES	35MM FOOTAGE	16MM FOOTAGE
1	1½	⅗	1	90	36
2	3	1⅕	2	180	72
3	4½	1⅘	3	270	108
4	6	2⅖	4	360	144
5	7½	3	5	450	180
6	9	3⅗	6	540	216
7	10½	4⅕	7	630	252
8	12	4⅘	8	720	288
9	13½	5⅖	9	810	324
10	15	6	10	900	360
11	16½	6⅗	11	990	396
12	18	7⅕	12	1080	432
13	19½	7⅘	13	1170	468
14	21	8⅖	14	1260	504
15	22½	9	15	1350	540
16	24	9⅗	16	1440	576
17	25½	10⅕	17	1530	612
18	27	10⅘	18	1620	648
19	28½	11⅖	19	1710	684
20	30	12	20	1800	720
21	31½	12⅗	21	1890	756
22	33	13⅕	22	1980	792
23	34½	13⅘	23	2070	828
24	36	14⅖	24	2160	864
25	37½	15	25	2250	900
26	39	15⅗	26	2340	936
27	40½	16⅕	27	2430	972
28	42	16⅘	28	2520	1008
29	43½	17⅖	29	2610	1044
30	45	18	30	2700	1080
31	46½	18⅗	31	2790	1116
32	48	19⅕	32	2880	1152
33	49½	19⅘	33	2970	1188
34	51	20⅖	34	3060	1224
35	52½	21	35	3150	1260
36	54	21⅗	36	3240	1296
37	55½	22⅕	37	3330	1332
38	57	22⅘	38	3420	1368
39	58½	23⅖	39	3510	1404
40	60	24	40	3600	1440
41	61½	24⅗	41	3690	1476
42	63	25⅕	42	3780	1512
43	64½	25⅘	43	3870	1548
44	66	26⅖	44	3960	1584
45	67½	27	45	4050	1620
46	69	27⅗	46	4140	1656
47	70½	28⅕	47	4230	1692
48	72	28⅘	48	4320	1728
49	73½	29⅖	49	4410	1764
50	75	30	50	4500	1800
51	76½	30⅗	51	4590	1836
52	78	31⅕	52	4680	1872
53	79½	31⅘	53	4770	1908
54	81	32⅖	54	4860	1944
55	82½	33	55	4950	1980
56	84	33⅗	56	5040	2016
57	85½	34⅕	57	5130	2052
58	87	34⅘	58	5220	2088
59	88½	35⅖	59	5310	2124
60	90	36	60	5400	2160

Fig. 2-4. Conversion chart, seconds of time to film footage.

The Stopwatch

In certain cases the conductor will elect to record his music without the film being projected. In this event, he relies on the stopwatch. This course is followed when a film is too compressed to allow the extra time for screening.

Regardless of whether the music is recorded while viewing the sequences on the screen or with the aid of the stopwatch, the music editor will normally mark the film with the guide indications which will later be of assistance to the music engineer during the dubbing period. And at the end of the sequence for which music is being recorded, either the diagonal line or series of punches will indicate where the music is to finish.

WRITING MUSIC TO TIMING

The composer will use as his guide the individual music cue sheet (Fig. 2-3) which has been prepared by the music editor. He will first consider any thematic material, either primary or subthematic, that he feels is necessary in his music plan. At certain points within a cue the indication might be that nonthematic music be written. The thematic music must then be molded or constructed so that there will be a smooth flow into and through the nonthematic sections, even though these sections may sometimes be in a different dramatic feeling. On the other hand, there will be times in which a definite atmospheric music change will be required. These sudden changes are used for shock effect, as indicators of a switch in locale or time, a shift in the dramatic exposition, and other situations that require music assistance. In all cases, however, balance and flow should be of uppermost importance. This marks the difference between the scores of the experienced professional and the amateur.

Using the Cue Sheets

The music cues will vary in length from 4-, 5-, or 6-second transitions to possible lengths of five minutes or more. Composers, in general, prefer to limit the duration of a music cue to 3−3½ minutes. In more lengthy sequences the composer will usually break the sequence into a series of shorter music cues. If we take, for example, a scene that lasts for nine minutes, it does not become too difficult to find strategic points in the extended scene to finish one piece of music and start a second, followed by even a third or fourth without the audience being aware that this is being done. The skill of the composer will manifest itself in the planning of the finish of one music sequence and overlapping another so that it will become a perfect unit whose seams are unnoticeable in the final presentation.

If we take, for example, a sequence of 3 minutes, 11 seconds (3:11), there can very easily be included variations in emotional feeling, dramatic reactions, changes of pace, and other functional elements that will need to be taken into consideration musically. Many of these might indicate a different tempo or pulsation of the music. The timing notations that the composer will indicate on his sketch will indicate points where the character of the music will change.

In a closer detailed description we might hypothetically say that the music cue sheet guide will, at the beginning (:00), relate a dialog scene between the male and female leads of the story. This scene probably had been selected to be

Fig. 2-5. Music sketch with timing variations.

accompanied by music because of certain dramatic emotion which it contained. The first point the composer will consider will be the tempo of the music: it must have substance without interfering with the dialog. A second point that he will consider will be whether any thematic music will be necessary in the scene. Thematic or nonthematic, the tempo will be most important.

A fairly safe rule of thumb would be either a tempo of three seconds (:03) or four seconds (:04) per $^4/_4$ bar. The composer may, in his concept, wish to vary the $^4/_4$ bar structure and include $^2/_4$, $^3/_4$, $^5/_4$ or $^6/_4$ bars in order to avoid a sense of monotony by continuing a long series of bars with 4 beats. In these instances the timings on his music sketch will have to compensate for extensions or contractions in the duration of 4 seconds per 4 beat bar. The deduction, therefore, would be quite simple in that a $^3/_4$ bar would consume 3 seconds, a $^5/_4$ bar 5 seconds, etc. A bit more complicated is when his primary tempo is 3 seconds per $^4/_4$ bar. The $^2/_4$ bar would then last for 1½ seconds, the $^5/_4$ bar approximately 3⅔ seconds, and the $^6/_4$ bar 4½ seconds. His music sketch would then appear as shown in Fig. 2-5.

In addition to this, the composer may wish to vary the tempo at certain points in order to give more freedom of expression. *Rallentandos* (relaxations of tempo), *accelerandos* (tempo increases), and *fermatas* (sustained notes or chords)—all must be taken into account in the timing structure.

The *rallentando* is noted in bar 3 of Fig. 2-6 with the timing compensation of 0:04 allowed for decreasing the tempo. Then, in bar 4 the music returns to the original tempo with the timing of 0:03 per bar as in the first two bars. Bar 5 calls for an increase in the tempo and allows 0:02 with a return again to the original tempo in bar 6. The *fermata* in bar 7 allows 0:04 with a further return to the original tempo in bar 8.

To continue with our referenced music cue sheet, let us assume that the dialog scene would finish at 0:55 and be followed by a dissolve to a highway with automobiles passing, which transition would last 0:05, followed by a dissolve to a gasoline station exterior with a car driving up to one of the pumps. We will assume that the male driver has been established as the villain in the story. The dialog could be that

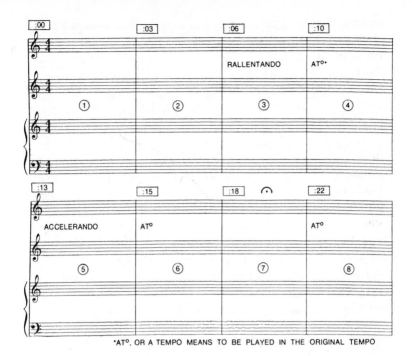

Fig. 2-6. Music sketch with tempo designations.

of ordering gasoline and asking for directions to a town some distance away. This scene would probably last :28 and end with the car pulling out. The previous highway transition scene would indicate an increased tempo in the music to possibly :02 per bar. The reason for the increase in tempo: (1) the accepted and expected music accompanying traffic is usually indicative of the realistic pace of the traffic, and (2) to assume a transition from one dramatic sequence or locale to another.

The music sketch would therefore be planned so that the change in music character would appear at :55 with possibly a further quality change (the dissolve to the gasoline pumps) at one minute (1:00). This change of approach is indicated because we have had music playing for realism during the short traffic scene and now it should prepare for the dialog to follow.

The composer will not necessarily lay out his music sketch so that the changes in the character of the music will appear at the beginning of bars where these changes occur. If the music idea has definite continuity the changes in tendency could very easily fall within a given bar of music.

With reference to timing indications, the question may arise as to why music cue sheets, in the majority of cases, designate timings in thirds of a second whereas it is not unusual in sketches or scores to find timings in half-seconds. The answer lies in the fact that the music editor will calculate the timings from footages. Many conductors, on the other hand, are more comfortable in following the stopwatch at half-second intervals. The exceptions are in cases of critical areas to be met with accents, punctuations, or changes of motivation, any of which may be designated in thirds of a second. This can only be solved with precision in one of two ways. Either with the use of a click loop or track, or recording with the aid of projected film which has been marked with streamers or punch marks at these points. If the stopwatch is used, the net result cannot be guaranteed to be exact in meeting the timings as set forth in the music cue sheet.

Drafting the Sketch

Printed sketch paper is typically used, with the rough music outline written on one, two, three, or more staves. The timings, taken from the music cue sheets, will be noted at the bars where they will fall, dependent on the tempo of the music that the composer has in mind. Isolated indications of instrumentation will possibly be noted. This writing, in the majority of cases, is done with pencil, because the eraser, which I feel is next in importance to the stopwatch, will undoubtedly be used to a great extent.

In this formative period, the sketch-drafting approach by composers will be varied (Fig. 2-7). Some will write a fragmentary one-stave sketch which they alone will be able to decipher as they develop their thoughts. Others will set down a fairly complete sketch, but with certain fine details not included. Still others will from the beginning include all instrument designations, dynamics, expression, and tempo marks—a condensed orchestral score. David Grusin goes directly from a very rough sketch to the orchestra score "unless I am working with an orchestrator, in which case I will then write a complete sketch."

Fig. 2-7. Incomplete music sketch, with instrument designations.

Alex North does his writing immediately into a six- or seven-staved sketch. He says: "It is practically an orchestral score and in many cases could be extracted by the copyist."

We should add to this that there have been a limited number of composers, apparently very confident and brave, who have bypassed the sketch procedure and from the beginning written directly into the score—with *ink*.

The reason for the sketch procedure is that it allows the composer to make any changes, alterations, elaborations, or polished developments of his original conception. In appearance it can be a simple melodic line or a very elaborate piece of unplayable piano music. (The composer will be writing for the orchestra, and this encompasses much more than can be performed with but ten fingers on a keyboard.)

The ultimate objective is the complete orchestral score. And achieving this involves several people: the *composer*, the *orchestrator*, and the *copyist*. The composer is the creator of the music. The orchestrator transcribes the music, originally written in the sketch, into the orchestral score. This score is written on printed sheets of music paper (Fig. 2-8) with the names of all of the instruments of the orchestra printed in the left margin adjacent to a music staff. These staves are usually divided into four bars per page. The copyist extracts the music from the score onto separate sheets for each instrument.

On preprinted scoring sheets, *flutes* occupy the top staves, followed by *oboes*, *clarinets*, *bassoons*, *horns*, etc. In further analysis, the instruments will be "written for" in their respective staves on each succeeding page. This is contrary to the structure of a printed page of piano music, which is presented vertically from the top of the page to the bottom. The reason for this difference is that the orchestral score will be used primarily by the conductor during the rehearsal and performance. He will be able to see at a glance what each instrument is playing in any given bar.

ORCHESTRATION

The orchestrator will complete the music score from the sketch, in perfect detail, indicating all written directions desired by the composer for the performance of his music.

At this point we must bring out certain variations that can occur in the process of composing and orchestrating. In most cases, with very few exceptions, composers are excellent orchestrators. The reason for the employment of a separate person to orchestrate the music is usually the time element, which would not allow one person to perform both functions. Where economy is indicated, with a narrow time span—in

Fig. 2-8. Music scoring sheet. (Note instrument names in left margin.)

other words, virtually always in practice—the composer will orchestrate his own music, in many cases from his rough sketch. Not all composers employ the orchestration procedure. In the case of Alex North and others, the sketch will be written in such fine detail that it can be passed directly to the copyist, thus bypassing orchestration entirely. (See Fig. 2-9.)

Fig. 2-9. Some composers prepare a detailed sketch, which may be turned over to the copyist.

Jerry Goldsmith and his orchestrator, Arthur Morton, work on a plan of detailed sketching in the beginning phases of the writing and as the work progresses the sketches may become more fragmentary because Morton has acquired an understanding of what the overall plan is and can continue the process with the desired result.

On the surface, the function of the orchestrator may seem mechanical: writing onto a score page what the composer has originally written in his sketch. But expert orchestrators can be of great assistance to composers in suggesting colors, additions of instrumental nuances, and other subtleties which contribute to the perfection of the overall music sound. The orchestrator can view the written music objectively, and this can be a huge advantage.

INSTRUMENTATION

There is a great variance in the complements of the orchestras used by film composers. With the addition of so many electronic and percussion instruments, composers who make use of only the more conventional studio orchestral instruments are in the minority. Originally, studio orchestral personnel were assembled after the manner of a symphony orchestra, though their numbers were fewer. Under unusual circumstances—high-budget extravaganzas, epics, one-time "specials"—a modified or full symphony orchestra might be used. Routinely, however, the normal studio orchestra averages between 35 and 60 musicians. And for low-budget films, this number drops to 15 or 20, or even less.

ARRANGING

An arrangement is literally a transcription of a piece of music from one medium to another, usually with certain embellishments.

One of the most noted and foremost arrangers in the popular music field was Ferde Grofé (*Grand Canyon Suite*), whose work for the early Paul Whiteman orchestra can only be considered a major contribution to that group's success as well as to the advancement of primitive jazz music.

There is a notable distinction between *orchestration* and *arranging*. The orchestrator transcribes the original composition into orchestral form without harmonic or melodic elaborations; the arranger will be expected to contribute, by invention, individual colors, rhythms, paraphrases, countermelodies, and other dressing in order to enhance but still preserve the original music concept. The arranger in a sense becomes a cocomposer of the basic piece of music.

Do not infer that orchestrators are incapable of arranging. In truth, many orchestrators and composers have had their initial training as arrangers, only to progress to composition or orchestration.

Arrangements of film music are generally associated with musicals, such as *Music in the Air*, *Fiddler on the Roof*, *An American in Paris*, Ross Hunter's version of *Lost Horizon*, *The King and I*, and countless other films that contained, at times, very involved and extensive dancing sequences, songs, and other music based on given themes.

Arranging, however, is not confined to the visual presentation of songs, dance sequences, etc. Arrangements may also constitute variations of nonvisual music themes in romantic, dramatic, comedy, and other films that employ a main or prime theme. An excellent example of this was *Love is a Many Splendored Thing*, in which Alfred Newman constructed many paraphrases of Sammy Fain's original song, in keeping with the dramatic sense but still preserving the basic melodic outline.

This function, therefore, although closely knit to both composition and orchestration, is an individual talent. It would be impossible to estimate the number of popular songs that have depended almost entirely upon some arrangement for their success. Of the songs that Cole Porter wrote for *Jubilee* in 1935, the immediate successes were undoubtedly *Just One of Those Things* and *Why Shouldn't I*. It wasn't until three years later that Artie Shaw recorded an arrangement of one of the lesser songs in the show, *Begin the Beguine*, and his arrangement undoubtedly contributed greatly to its inclusion in the popular standard repertoire of all-time smash hits.

Songwriters who have not the ability to write notes on paper (Irving Berlin was one) depend completely on the arranger to draft the original music as well as arrange for orchestral or vocal rendition.

64

COPYING

The copyist—a combination of musician, artist, and craftsman—is involved in transcribing or extracting the written notes from the orchestral score to separate pages of music for each instrument in the orchestra. The score page, as defined before, is written in horizontal fashion with each instrument's notes occupying its given staff on each page. The copyist or *extractor* of this music will write a separate page of music for each instrument, written vertically, similar to a piece of piano music.

Ideally, the copyist should be capable of detecting any errors that might occur in the orchestral score. During the period of copying the individual parts, he will be expected to scan the score page as he copies each part in order to ferret out little mistakes and flag any major discrepancies.

At times the copyist may be called upon to write a *conductor* part, which is a condensation of the score, usually on four, five, or six staves, for the use of the conductor during recording. This condensed score may be copied from the composer's sketch; but since this sketch generally does not contain enough detail, he normally makes the extraction from the full score.

In copying the individual parts, the copyist exercises great care so that there can be no doubt in any musician's mind at the time of recording. Many copyists take pride in producing handwritten sheets that very closely approximate printed music in appearance.

Ordinarily the copyist will assume the responsibility of librarian, the custodian of the copied music parts from the finish of this endeavor up to the time and place of the recording.

The copyist attends the recording session in order to correct any errors that might have occurred during the extraction as well as to make any possible necessary alterations in the parts.

Instruments and Their Character

There was a time when all of the major studios had under contract a set group of 35–45 musicians. The grouping would typically consist of at least 2 flutes, 1 oboe (also playing English horn), 2 clarinets (possibly also playing saxophones), 1 bass clarinet (playing also clarinet and possibly saxophone), 2 French horns, 4 trumpets, 4 trombones (one playing bass trombone), 2 percussion (drummers), 1 harp, 1 piano, 1 guitar, 8 violins, 2 violas, 2 celli, 1 string bass.

In low-budget productions, selection of the 15–20 musicians was always a problem. In order to satisfactorily score a dramatic or western film with the conventional woodwind, brass, and strings, a certain musical "weight" is required, particularly for the wide-screen or "panoramic" films. All sorts of trick combinations of musicians were thought up by composers. Films were scored with only a single guitar; or all brass instruments (the very thought of which brings to mind a brass band); or groupings of all strings; or woodwind.

There was a degree of success and even a few notable successes, as in the case of *Harry Lime's Theme*, played on the zither, in *The Third Man*. (This experience led to a rash of films using only solo instruments for the music score, none of which duplicated this profitable accomplishment.)

The instrumentation that the present-day film composer will use for his score will first be governed by the budget allowed for the music. If he has accepted a fixed-fee contract, his own arithmetic will dictate the size of the group. Once this decision has been made, he will consider which instruments he will use in this grouping. The type of film—dramatic, western, comedy, historic, extravaganza, horror, science fiction—will suggest the basic combination of instruments; but this is only a suggestion. There is no set rule as to what the musical grouping should be. In a space opera one composer may choose a more or less standard basic orchestra and depend upon his writing and the many available effects in recording and dubbing to give the music a stellar quality. Another composer may decide to use only electronics (it was successful in *Forbidden Planet*).

In the quest for a "different" sound, many producers have encouraged excessive experimentation; this at the expense of colors available in a well balanced group. Using as a basis percussion and electronics, composers will often, either by reason of budget or personal preference, neglect the proportions of balance and settle for the addition of only brass and woodwinds, including possibly saxophones.

Even in the use of conventional instruments certain "excesses" can occur. Consider the alto, or bass flute, which is a larger version of the conventional flute and produces a deeper tone. Some composers, enthralled by its low sonorous sound, have employed two or three of these instruments playing in unison in the lower register to generate weird or sensuous melodic passages. The coupling of more than one instrument in unison (playing the same notes or passage) is not necessarily intended to produce a greater volume. Each individual player will produce a sound from his instrument in a slightly different timbre, different vibrato, different tone. This creates a music effect which, when used economically, *can be* very attractive; however, these solo instruments or multiples of the same instrument can, by overuse, be likened to too much syrup on a sundae. Excesses often occur in the use of bongos, electronic instruments, muted brass, and other instruments that produce an unusual sound. Perhaps a good watchword for instrument selection would be *temperance*. Let us examine the scope of sounds available in a conventional orchestral ensemble.

INSTRUMENTAL LIMITATIONS

During the creating process, the composer usually has definite instruments in mind; and he writes for them music *that is within their scope of performance.* He must know the technical limits of execution of each instrument, be able to "hear" mentally the different sounds in their respective registers as well as all of the varied colors that are possible with mixed groupings of instruments. Only with this basic knowledge can he expect to turn out a score that proves in its performance what he intended in his composition.

Table 3-1 lists the more common emotional or atmospheric qualities with their "compatible" instrument associations.

WOODWINDS

In the conventional orchestra's woodwind section are the flautist (who will also play piccolo and alto flute), the oboist (playing also the English horn), and musicians who play the B-flat clarinet and the bassoon. It is not uncommon to use two flautists, one or both playing piccolo and alto flute; and two or three B-flat clarinetists, one or more playing also bass clarinet and possibly saxophone. A further possibility with the clarinet group is the E-flat alto clarinet, an instrument that is very seldom used. It has a lovely midrange tone between the B-flat clarinet and the bass clarinet, and can be very useful not only as a solo instrument but playing with, and thereby fortifying, the violas.

With regard to the oboe, more than one will be used only in larger groups, usually of 40 or more musicians.

A still further distinctive-sound possibility in the clarinet group is the contrabass clarinet with its low, deep, guttural sound, used often in mystery or horror films. It is pitched one octave lower than the bass clarinet.

As with the contrabass clarinet, the bassoon player will often be called upon to perform on the contrabassoon, which also has a very low, reedy, guttural buzz in its tone. It too is pitched one octave lower than the normal bassoon.

BRASS

The brass group includes trumpet, trombone, French horn, euphonium, and tuba or bass horn. The B-flat trumpet

Table 3-1. Mood Categories and Associated Instruments.

QUALITY	INSTRUMENTS
DRAMA	Low strings French horns or trombones Low woodwinds English horn (low register) Bass flute (low register) Contrabass clarinet (low register) Piano
MYSTERY	Low flute Strings (tremolando) Contrabassoon (low register) French horns (stopped or muted) Novachord or Hammond organ Yamaha organ Moog synthesizer
ROMANCE	Violins (middle and high register) B-flat Clarinet (middle register) Oboe (with caution) Flute (middle register) Bass flute (middle and low register) French horn (middle and high register) Bass clarinet (high register) Violas, celli (middle and high register) Vibraphone
HUMOR	Bassoon (middle and low register) Oboe (middle and high register) Clarinet (all registers) Xylophone Bass clarinet (low)
SCENIC (PASTORAL)	Flute (middle and high register) Horn (middle and high register) Trumpet (middle register) Clarinet (middle register) English horn (middle register) Oboe (middle and high register) Violins (high register) Harp (middle and high register) Piano (middle and high register)
SCIENCE FICTION	Moog synthesizer Yamaha organ Female soprano voice Vibraphone (haze effects) Many percussion effects Strings (harmonics) Flute (high register)
HORROR	Contrabass clarinet Contrabassoon Tuba Low trombones Electronic instruments (effects) Piano (low, bass clef) French horns (low register, stopped) Tympani Bass drum
NARRATIVE BACKGROUND	Combined strings and woodwind (middle register)

player is rarely asked to play another instrument, although in isolated cases he may be requested to play a C trumpet, pitched higher than the B-flat trumpet. The French horn player will play only his given instrument. One of the trombonists will be expected to play the B-flat bass trombone, a lower pitched instrument whose compass allows it to be played six tones lower than the normal B-flat trombone. The euphonium is usually reserved for brass bands and is rarely if ever used in studio recording orchestras. The tuba or upright

Table 3-2. Instruments and Their Associated Qualities.

INSTRUMENTS	HIGH REGISTER	MIDDLE REGISTER	LOW REGISTER
FLUTE	PANORAMIC SCENIC BRIGHT & GAY	ROMANTIC SUBTLE	MYSTERIOUS SUBTLE
ALTO FLUTE BASS FLUTE	WEAK VOLUME (NOT RECOMMENDED)	DRAMATIC MYSTERIOUS OMINOUS	DRAMATIC WEAK OMINOUS
OBOE	THIN PLAINTIVE	IMPRESSIVE ASSERTIVE HUMOROUS	DRAMATIC SUSPENSEFUL
ENGLISH HORN	THIN APPEALING	STRONG LONESOME FOREBODING	DARK VIVID
BASSOON	THIN PLAINTIVE	FORCEFUL MELODIC MYSTERIOUS DRAMATIC	DRAMATIC HUMOROUS
CONTRABASSOON	NOT RECOMMENDED	LITTLE EFFECT	ENIGMATIC SCARY MYSTERIOUS SINISTER
B-FLAT CLARINET	STRONG ASSERTIVE	MELODIC ROMANTIC	DARK WARM
BASS CLARINET	APPEALING MELODIC	WARM	DRAMATIC DARK HUMOROUS
CONTRABASS CLARINET	LITTLE EFFECT	MYSTERIOUS DRAMATIC	MELODRAMATIC OMINOUS
FRENCH HORN	ASSERTIVE FORCEFUL	WARM APPEALING	DRAMATIC
TRUMPET	HEROIC STRONG INDEPENDENT ASSERTIVE	MELODIC FORCEFUL INDIVIDUALISTIC	DRAMATIC NOSTALGIC
TROMBONE	MELODIOUS HEAVY	STRONG DRAMATIC	DARK MELODRAMATIC SOMBER
VIOLINS	SPIRITED MELODIC ARRESTING	WARM ROMANTIC COMPASSIONATE	DARK DRAMATIC MOROSE
VIOLAS	THIN MELODIC	WARM MELLOW NOSTALGIC	DARK DRAMATIC
CELLI	TENSE ROMANTIC	WARM SONOROUS	DRAMATIC ASSERTIVE

bass horn is not generally used in studio orchestras except with large groups, and particularly in connection with extravaganzas or military-type films.

PERCUSSION

The instruments used in the percussion or drum section are almost too numerous to set down. One of the leading authorities on the many instruments available for use in the percussion section is Emil Richards, whose book *World of Percussion* lists 300 standard, ethnic, and special percussion instruments and effects. These instruments have had a profound effect on film music creation. The introduction of new and unusual percussion effects into the standard orchestral sound has indeed been of vital importance in altering the basic concept of film scoring.

The standard percussion instruments such as drums, cymbals, tympani, orchestra bells, and the like have now been supplemented by not only a host of latin instruments but many exotic instruments from India, Burma, Japan, Bali, and other places.

Use of the more unconventional instruments is not necessarily relegated to association only with the countries of their origin. All are used freely in establishing different color values when coupled with standard orchestral sounds. A case in point is the tambourine, which for many years was associated with Spanish and gypsy dancing and is now an accepted part of the rhythm section in modern jazz music. This also applies to bongo drums (Cuban), conga drums (Afro-Cuban), and tom-toms (American Indian).

In essence, the application of any percussive sound that might enhance an existing instrumental color is acceptable.

STRINGS

The string section is composed of violin, viola, cello, and string bass or contrabass.

The four primary instrument families, then, are the woodwinds, brass, percussion, and strings. To these we might add the harp, piano and celeste, the guitar, and the saxophone family (E-flat or C soprano, E-flat alto, C melody, the B-flat tenor, E-flat baritone, and the B-flat bass).

ELECTRONIC INSTRUMENTS

Some educational, documentary, industrial, cartoon, outer-space fantasies, and avant garde films are logical subjects for the application of the special sounds achievable with electronic instruments. The sounds of electronic instruments, however, assume solo tone quality, which will not blend readily with more conventional orchestra instruments. These sounds will immediately attract attention as a "foreign" tonal element. Certain exceptions do occur, particularly in the use of the Novachord or Hammond organ with small instrumental groups. With intelligent application these electronic instruments can be quite successful in reinforcing smaller combinations of instruments.

A case in point is the nonelectric harpsichord. The early use of this instrument by Bach, Haydn, and Mozart was for solo purposes. The later development of the piano relegated it also to solo status.

The recent "electrification" of both harpsichord and piano has actually increased the solo possibilities as well as the percussive qualities of these instruments.

Unfortunately, not all instrument sounds have been enhanced by the application of electronic amplification. Certain string sounds, for example, have been destructively augmented by introduction of excessive tonal distortion.

At present, electronic accessories are available for almost any instrument in the orchestra. The occasional use of these in orchestral scoring can add a unique and interesting character to some compositions. However, these curiosities have seemed, to a great many composers, much too attractive for only moderate use.

I approached six prominent film composers to comment on the uses of electronics. Hugo Friedhofer finds them valuable as an additional tool, but does not like them "as a substitute for existing instruments":

> "The man who in a way was the founding father of this type of sound was Edgar Varese, who managed somehow to make electronic sounds with perfectly normal instruments long before electronics crept in. Later, however, he did utilize electronics, specifically in the piece of music that he wrote for the Brussels International Fair in 1958. He said, putting it altruistically: *Just because we have the automobile there is no reason for killing the horse.*"

73

Alex North, when asked if he felt that electronic instruments were being used excessively, had this comment:

"Perhaps I haven't seen too many films that have used electronics, but the few that I have seen indicates that this type of approach has been overextended...I think it's time to get back to what I have tried to do—achieving, through the legitimate orchestra, a simulated sound of electronics.

"It is possible that I was the first one to use electronics in 1940. I was fascinated with the Novachord but was unable to locate one for use in my score for *Spartacus*. I then used the *ondioline*, a French instrument. I'm not against the use of electronic instruments if they are integrated and make sense."

David Grusin suggests that use of electronic sounds is cyclic:

"When the synthesizer was first made available out here, Paul Beaver had the franchise and everybody ran down there and found out a few basic facts of life about it. It was going to be the solution to all of our scoring problems. Then there was a year when it became very hip not to use it. Now I think the synthesizer has settled into being just one of many music elements to use. I think that it's being handled more judiciously now than at the beginning. The same is true with all of the others. I very much like ethnic instruments. I love the projects that allow you to use them.

"As to electronic music, I feel that there is something very sympathetic between electronically produced sound and film. I don't know why that is. It's possibly because they are both synthetic media. Something seems to work with well written and well recorded electronic music."

John Green was asked, with the availability of so many new and exotic electronic and percussion instruments, *Do you feel that many composers cannot resist the temptation to experiment too much with these different colors?* His reply:

"I think the question is unfortunate because I would have to be told what is too much. I think the unwillingness to experiment with, the unwillingness to learn about new sources of usable music sounds would be a real malaise. On the other hand, I think the employment of those sounds for the sheer sake of employing a gimmick is also a malaise. In my own case I have been told that I used the Moog synthesizer very effectively in the main title of *They Shoot Horses, Don't They?*. I haven't used it since. Electronic music should be used only where it is dramatically valid—not just because it is a new sound."

Do some composers tend to misuse the many available unorthodox, strange sounding, or exotic percussion instruments? Quincy Jones thinks so:

"I guess all of us have been guilty of it at one time or another. I've always had a tendency to try just a little smidge of sound before I just dive in and fall in love with trying to revolutionize the violin. As to the synthesizer, I think that I used it first in the theme for *Ironside*. It was so subliminal, just down front. We used it only for identifying sound and like garlic salt rather than potatoes.

"You can go crazy with Vibraslaps. They're very rich sounds and I think that I like it best fused with the orchestra rather than trying to make a down-front sound. I like it as another instrument in the orchestra."

Does he feel that misusage is an attempt to create new colors by reason of many TV orchestras being limited to brass, woodwind, and rhythm—or is it used for sensationalism?

"Both! Most of the time composers trying to break through feel that a new color is sensational. It's going to be their identifying trademark. I think that overindulgence comes from just that. Also, you'd be surprised how a lot of producers are. At a recording a producer will come out of the booth and say, *'What is that?'* 'Why, that's a three-tit bassoon from Malaya.' *'Really?'*... They put the guys on with that kind of thing—and themselves, to replace quality. They really know what's happening with the Moog synthesizer. It's ridiculous. Like they're clarinet players. After all, it's another instrument in the orchestra and takes a lot of judgment in its use."

Arthur Morton was questioned about the use of new and unusual sounds in films—are they the result of newer recording techniques, such as multiple tracks, overlays, delayed reverberation, etc?

"A lot of that is old technique. Most of it is the electronic instruments themselves. The electric flute, the electric clarinet, the electric trumpet; you can put the fuzz (tone distortion) on them similar to the way it is done with the electric guitar. This all helps to create these new unusual sounds if used intelligently. They were used in *Patton* with much imagination by Jerry Goldsmith. He has always been three years ahead of the rest in the use of electronics. The use of Echoplex (electronic attachment) on the flute makes the instrument sound a repeated phrase with a long fade or decay, like fading off into the distance. It can be attached to the harp as well as other instruments. The sound is produced through a loudspeaker. It gives all of the effects that can be done with the electric guitar.

"Instead of using these devices as a crutch, however, they should only be used as an addition to the dramatic score. With due respect to these electronics and their versatility and value, they still do not take the place of music. Their best use is when they are used as music. Their misuse is not productive because it's in the hands of primitives who are overcome with the paraphernalia rather than having an actual concern for the music *per se*."

Another point to be considered is that to fully understand and be aware of the wide range of potential in electronics demands much time and study. Many present-day film composers either do not have the time for extensive exploration or are satisfied with the more conventional types of electronic sounds.

Organs and Synthesizers

Electronic organs primarily deal with fixed sounds and are completely polyphonic. Synthesizers essentially are a one note instrument at any given time. Multiples of the one note are possible to form a chord, but if one plays up and down the keyboard, this chord structure will follow mechanically in parallel motion. (Some recent synthesizers have been modified to play two notes.)

Synthesizers are basically designed to allow a person to produce any sound he can imagine. As against the organ, with its bassoon, flute, horn, and other stops, the synthesizer can be programed, with proper filters, envelope generators, etc. to duplicate these sounds.

In *The War Between Men and Women*, Marvin Hamlish wanted a sound that combined the sounds of wind blowing, a flute, and a recorder. It was achieved on a synthesizer. In a recent film that Henry Mancini scored he had gong sounds synthesized that were impossible to produce in the percussion section. He also asked for a polite double-reed sound (oboe or English horn). This was also produced on a synthesizer. The synthesizer is an instrument that produces not only sound effects but music sounds that are impossible to achieve by any other single music instrument.

In the area of sound effects, a similarity does exist between organs and synthesizers: both have the ability to produce such sound effects as jet planes, thunder, explosions, wind, storms, rain, etc.

The early pioneers in producing abstract music by utilizing electronic tone generators were Perry and Kingsley, who produced these sounds by recording individual tones on magnetic tape and then splicing the tones together. This laborious and inefficient method inspired Robert A. Moog and Donald Buchla to develop electronic synthesizers which would circumvent the primitive tape splicing procedure. Both men completed their endeavors and produced voltage controlled sounds with their respective synthesizers.

The Moog (pronounced $\overline{mog}$) synthesizer uses a keyboard controller which can be calibrated to play tempered scales. Buchla's device uses touch sensors rather than a keyboard controller. The Moog is perhaps more easily adaptable to tonal music, shereas the Buchla points toward the more unusual sound possibilities depending upon the ingenuity of the operator.

Constructing the
Music Score

The form an original music score will take is dependent upon many factors, not the least of which is the type of production—drama, comedy, mystery, western, detective, intrigue, spy, monster, period....Each of these must be further subclassified, too. The requirements for a sophisticated adult comedy would differ considerably from those for a buffoonesque slapstick diversion.

The only real guide to the music approach is a broad formula that relies on use of set patterns that have become familiar to the audience in association with normal or routine scenes or situations.

In the case of the western, we can expect, at times, scenic photography, gunplay, hard riding, stalking or chase sequences, the inevitable barroom, and usually innocuous romance. Most westerns, being of a certain period, become in a sense a documentary of sorts because of the locales and dates of the story.

History has given us the type of music that was performed in this era as well as instruments that were used. Usually fiddle, accordian or concertina, banjo or guitar, and an occasional out-of-tune barroom piano. Although it is not probable that any group of musicians during this period carried around a huge bass viol, the license has been taken by film composers in adding this instrument to give more depth, undoubtedly, to the music recording.

Therefore, the tone and nature of the music will usually be predicated by these sounds if it is intended to be realistic. Even if there are no visual scenes of such instruments, a sense of western feeling will many times make the use of these instruments desirable in the course of the music scoring. In some cases, a square-dance rhythm and tempo will be imitated without the use of these basic instruments but the general flavor will be retained by the standard orchestra.

Where the composer will allow himself to stray from the established western sound will be in the scenic or *pastoral* and dramatic sequences. But even here we find certain precedents being followed. It is expected that wide, lush landscapes will be accompanied by the large orchestral sound, imitating the scope of the photography as much as possible. The curious fact remains that many times the composer will not examine the possibility of remoteness and lonesomeness in such scenes and write the music accordingly. It might be wiser to use solo instruments, properly written for such as the clarinet or trumpet—to give this sense of remoteness and thus enhance the photography to a greater extent. John Ford has many times called for this approach. And Hugo Friedhofer says, "A perfect example of scenic or pastoral descriptive music is the opening of Aaron Copland's *Billy the Kid*."

Of course, everything depends upon the dramatic motivation, but one must take into consideration the wisdom of allowing the music to compete with scenic photography.

The same situation would be present in the approach to hard riding, the chase, and roundup or stampede sequences. The accepted formula here has been the use of imitative orchestral sounds in combination with realistic sound effects. In this case there is just too little dynamic area on the sound track to accept this competition. Consequently, something has to be subordinate—usually, it is music. The suggestion here would be to consider the overall strength and weight of the sound effects and, even more so, the strength and weight of the drama itself. If the combination of the two forces has enough dynamic quality, the sequence might very well have enough impetus to call for no music at all.

A good example is the *wolf hunt* sequence in the Russian film *War and Peace*. This extended-length section of the film was presented in its entirety with no music and a minimum of sound effects. The pace of the action, which included above-average editing, indicated that the addition of music and sound effects would be unnecessary.

If there is a noticeable lack of strength in the dramatic exposition, the approach should be to bolster this lack and not compete with thundering hooves. In the case of a glorified, exciting, nondramatic chase or roundup, it might be advisable to allow the evident rhythmic impulses of the realism to become the basic rhythm of the music and write to this with possibly only the higher areas of the orchestra—violins, woodwinds and trumpets—exemplifying the excitement.

More latitude is, of course, allowed in nonwestern films, with the possible exception of such historic *period* films as Arabian Nights fantasies, 18th and 19th century costume films, Revolutionary war and Civil war sagas, and the like. However, with these historic films a degree of freedom is acceptable as long as the era is preserved musically in the basic approach. Nevertheless, this does not mean that the composer will limit himself to only the music sounds and instruments inherent to any particular period. Rather, he will interweave his score with enough historic or period substance, usually imitative, to give credence to the overall music tapestry. It would be unthinkable to approach a film story with an historic Eastern locale by using only authentic Chinese music, which is generally unacceptable to the Occidental ear. This would also apply to East Indian music, with its use of quarter-tones, as well as to Arabian, which is extremely limited in melodic scope due to the music scale structure that comprises fewer notes than our diatonic scale.

The overall concept of the production in the script will dictate the original music plan, not in terms of actual notes on paper but the general feel or tenor to be developed by the music score. We may, however, find conflicting elements at this point. What may seem to be an out and out simple dramatic exposition may, after thorough examination, and after photography, have hidden or subtle facets that can change the concept completely. The script can give only so much information: dialog, camera angles, dissolves, fadeouts, and other technical data.

At its best, the guide is a cold one, to be given life by the director and film editor, and necessitating emotional contribution by the music. A series of scenes involving a murder may *seem to* indicate dramatic music building to the murder climax when, after photography and editing, there may be some compassion due the murderer which can be heightened musically.

As a consequence, the original idea or plan should be rough and flexible to the extent that it can be ultimately altered as necessary to be of greatest benefit to the dramaturgy.

In the Spring 1972 issue of *American Cinemeditor*, Alfred Perry, music supervisor of **Four Star International, Inc.**, says:

> "The contemporary use of background music is designed to help satisfy the audience's curiosity. It addresses itself to the emotional dimensions for which it is the best suited means of expression. After all, music can say without blushing what would be imprudent to verbalize. It can and it must probe the subconscious of the characters and disclose it in its own tactful language to the audience whenever the subconscious is material to the action of the characters."

Although the original music idea may seem confusing, there is a point of departure which is most often followed: the selection of a main theme for the production. It is possible that subthemes or *motifs* might be necessary, but the heavy concentration will be on the prime thematic music. The formula for achieving this varies to a certain extent.

It is not unusual for a producer or director to request more than one piece of thematic music from a composer and then make his choice of the one to be used. Composers in general do not favor this audition procedure. Alex North refuses outright to such multiple-theme submittal, claiming that his assignment is based on his background of successful film music and that the producer, in his decision to hire him, should understand that what he will write will be perfectly suited to the project.

Henry Mancini, in *Directors and Film Scores* (*Action* Magazine, Nov.–Dec. 1973), says:

> "The first title song in a dramatic picture that made sense and proved a commercial success was *High Noon* by Dimitri

Tiomkin. It pulled out the plug on everything. Now a composer is preconditioned to start work on a picture and expect a director or producer to ask for a title song. I have to tell them sometimes it works, sometimes it doesn't.

"On some films we've written complete songs, then did not use the lyrics because we felt they would serve no dramatic purpose. The minute you put a song over the titles or any part of the picture, you're trying to get people to listen, go out and buy. Often these songs don't progress the action or make a kind of comment. We had a title sone in *Charade*, which played under a boat scene and worked fairly well. It didn't go over the titles because the titles were not designed to take it.

"In *Two For the Road*, we had a song (lyrics by Leslie Bricusse) that had no place in the picture, so we agreed not to put it in. *Sunflower* also had a title song. Vittorio DeSica, Carlo Ponti, and I agreed to have it sung at the end. It was originally planned to be heard at the beginning, but it proved distracting.

"In *Days of Wine and Roses*, the title song worked just fine. Also, in *Dear Heart*. A couple others I've written have worked. It's simply a matter of whether the song fits with the story and mood, or whether you're doing it for pure exploitation."

Following the decision on the subject of the main theme any subthemes or motifs will probably be constructed by the composer. Rarely will the producer be interested in making decisions on these. The subtheme device is typically used to accompany recurring situations and possibly to accompany supporting players if the motivation of their character roles indicate such use, as well as other dramatic points that may need heightening for emphasizing the characterization or as shock value.

There are, of course, some films that do not call for a prime, expansive main theme. In cases such as these the leitmotif technique of fragmentary character-identifying music will usually be employed with proper variations and developments as the dramatics dictate.

On the thematic approach, Alex North had this to say:

"You can establish a very simple theme like I did in *Who's Afraid of Virginia Woolf?*. Only three notes. Then during certain scenes when the conflict became greater I distorted that particular music and gave it another kind of dimensional approach to fit the particular scene."

No two composers will ever create the basic music in exactly the same way. Their talent and craft will dictate the individualism that is so necessary in preserving the fresh, truly original music sounds, especially in theatrical films.

Insofar as television films and series are concerned, an unfortunate situation exists. The nature of this medium makes time of prime importance; this fact is responsible for the frequent duplications of approach.

In television series the thematic music is usually performed only at the opening and closing of each episode. This identifying music has been very successful commercially in many cases. Such musical offerings as those from *Mission Impossible*, *Dragnet*, *Ironside*, *Peter Gunn*, and other notable themes have enjoyed considerable phonograph record sales.

An interesting trend in many of the more recent series is that the identifying themes are rarely used to any extent in paraphrases or dramatic variations throughout the body of the episodes. A possible reason for this is the likelihood of more than one composer having been assigned to complete the music in a limited time.

With increasing frequency, one composer will be assigned to write the theme only, but his talents will not be employed in the actual scoring or dramatic writing. Quincy Jones, who wrote the themes for *The Bill Cosby Show*, *Ironside*, and *Sanford and Son*, wrote the dramatic music for the two-hour pilot and the first six episodes of *Ironside*, following which his comment was, "Jesus! This would kill you—put you in your grave! Especially if you write emotionally."

Occasionally in the program content of *Wild, Wild West* and *Star Trek*, references to the theme music have been detected, but these references never assumed much importance. In *Combat*, there have been more extensive thematic variations—undoubtedly because the greater part of the music for each episode was written by the composer of the identifying theme, Leonard Rosenman.

With *Mission Impossible* it is difficult to understand the heavy military use of percussion—almost to the point of being an irritant. The series was, after all, a "foreign intrigue" type with a short music theme, which could be more correctly termed a *motif*. In one episode, the military drums and large hand cymbals were used no less than 35 times! And the theme, a motif, was evident in the same episode 26 times.

DEVELOPING ORIGINAL IDEAS

The prime theme and subthemes are interwoven throughout the story development, with music of nonthematic structure. This nonthematic music is designed not only to heighten dramatic emotion, but to convey feelings or thoughts that cannot be told or presented through action and photography, and to serve as a signal for relating to past incidents and warnings of impending dramatic situations. In short, the nonthematic music provides the "hinge" for development of dramatic sequences.

The main theme will be used as a *connecting link* for the characters and situations with which it is associated. This development must be handled very carefully, and the skill of the composer will be manifest by the theme variations that he will be able to construct. No two dramatic or emotional scenes will be the same. In the plot development, the story context will undoubtedly contain emotional highs and lows that generally build to a climax of one form or another. With this in mind, it certainly would be unwise to create a set arrangement or version of the theme and depend upon this to carry through the entire story. Well planned descriptive variations for a story's many subtle emotional changes will, if anything, enhance the theme and dramaturgy more than constant repetition. This fact has been proved throughout music history. Opera, symphony, operetta, the musical and dramatic theatre—all have followed the unwritten-but-understood law of never giving the audience too much of a good thing: Leave them asking for more.

In opera the aria is rarely reprised. At times, audience demand has made it necessary to perform an encore of an aria, but this is not usual. Thematic repetition is more common in operetta; but even here the usual format is in reprise *versions*, without the full impact of the main, essential presentation.

Symphonies give us probably the greatest examples of the proper handling of thematic music: the main theme presentation followed by lesser subthemes interwoven with paraphrases, juxtapositions, variations of just enough references to the main theme to tease the audience until its development makes a climatic statement of the theme in its entirety. Much the same formula follows through in other music art forms.

An unfortunate situation exists today in the excessive use of given music themes in film production. The causes of this are manifold but we must assume that it is a direct reaction, conscious or unconscious, to an effect that television commercial jingles have on the public: These jingles are designed to sell products; and the theory has been that if the jingle is catchy and performed in saturation, the audience will have gone through a form of music brainwashing (a psychological association will be made automatically between a jingle and its product while the consumer shops in the supermarket).

This idea has carried over into film production and, as a consequence, we find more and more producers looking for the all important "big" theme to be used as much as possible throughout the photoplay.

One certainly cannot argue with the financial statistics of one composer's share in disc sales of his music score having already passed the million-dollar mark, but for one of these gigantic successes we could possibly find a dozen or two that returned but very modest royalties.

Attesting to the distressing absurdity of this situation is the fact that it has been common practice for some producers, after the music score has been recorded, to order many reprints of the main theme and replace perfectly valid and otherwise highly effective music with the theme.

Quincy Jones says:

> "I wrote a main title for a picture...and after the recording was finished the producer liked the theme so much that he said, 'Make me five copies of that,' and then threw out all of those difficult chases that I wrote and replaced them with the theme. It's maddening!"

Much the same situation was experienced by Jerry Goldsmith in his score for *The Blue Max*. Goldsmith's orchestrator, Arthur Morton, who in his own right is an excellent composer, relates:

> "...It was a marvelous score—wedded to the picture. The director, who was the strong man in this instance, fell in love with one tune and threw out many sequences and used this tune over and over. It was a beastly bore and did immeasurable harm to what the music could have meant to the film. ...Motion picture makers should stay in the motion picture business and use music as it helps the photoplay."

One can only assume that in the overextended use of a main theme, the producer's mind is probably dwelling on the "fast buck." People may well leave the theatre whistling the theme, but the longevity of all but a handful of these melodies will prove disappointingly short. Will they become part of standard popular music literature, such as Jerome Kern's *Why Was I Born?*, George Gershwin's *A Foggy Day*, Cole Porter's *Love For Sale*, Richard Rodgers' *Some Enchanted Evening*, and Arthur Schwartz' *Dancing in the Dark*? Not likely.

The use and development of subthemes or *motifs* does not suffer from the same fate of repetition as the principal theme except, of course, that they can be just as vulnerable to replacement due to the whims of the producer. The development of these all-important fragmentary pieces of music follows the plot development and can be of tremendous assistance to the enfoldment of the story. Here is where the composer will be able to make the greatest use of the many varied orchestral colors in either duplicating or adding further dimension to the existing plot situations. His knowledge of the sounds of the individual instruments and the emotions they best inspire is a most valuable tool. Added to this is the collective sound of combined instruments that gives him untold varieties of color to assist in these developments. All, of course, should be handled judiciously with only one thought—how best to assist and not impair the intended emotions or situations coming from the screenplay.

SOURCE MUSIC

In the course of witnessing a completed film and hearing the accompanying music all of us at times have been conscious of sound-effect music as against *functional* music that assists or complements dramatic action. A radio playing, either seen or implied, a dance band in a nightclub, a circus calliope, marching bands, or any other such story-related music is referred to as *source* music, meaning simply that it is being heard from a particular source.

This very important phase of film music construction may be dictated by the photographic source or implied in the depicted situation. A dialog scene in an automobile may not indicate dramatic scoring, but a music pace or tempo might still be desirable; therefore, the car radio could be playing, whether we see the radio or not.

Source music used to convey a specific feeling, or in establishing a foreign or historic locale, performs a dual role in that it serves a functional purpose as well. Selection of music for such purposes can present problems to the composer, and he may have to decide at times to abandon authenticity in favor of dramatic scoring, or present both realism and functional playing in juxtaposition at the same time, or add to the realism in order to heighten excitement. A lone singer in a canoe will be orchestrally supported, for example—though the audience realizes that musicians are not part of the plotted action.

A graphic example of intelligent handling of a difficult situation was a sequence in *Desire Under The Elms*. Elmer Bernstein was faced with a single hoedown fiddler playing for a strenuous dance by Burl Ives, which built to a feverish climax. As the dance progressed with the cast joining in, cuts were interjected that demanded dramatic scoring in direct contrast to the frenzy that was building in the dance. Bernstein had the lone fiddler playing at the start, and then imperceptibly added other instruments of the orchestra to build the excitement. Along with this he was able to instill heavy dramatic emotion during the cuts and still preserve the overall hoedown buildup to the climax.

Hugo Friedhofer relates his problems with source music in one of his film assignments:

> "In *The Sun Also Rises* there was much source music and a great deal of overlapping of different brass bands and sounds of various kinds. I was working with Alexander Courage. who is an expert on bullfight music and traditional music sounds. We sat with that thing and worked out a blueprint before ever thinking about a note of music. Deciding just at which point one heard a band approaching from screen left crossing to screen right and another band crossing from screen right to screen left—also at which point a certain instrumental group of purely native (off-screen) source music should be heard. and where it should disappear. Furthermore. where we should go from pure underscoring into source music."

Source music will be either prerecorded or added following photography. If the composer is faced with a nightclub scene and a handful of dance-band musicians performing, a degree of latitude is allowed in recording music, to match the band, with a reasonably larger orchestra. In cases such as this the director can be of assistance in photographing angles that do not pinpoint the small group but imply that more musicians are included, but not seen by the camera.

With source music being played from radios or hi-fi sets, the type of music applied could be compatible with the story line and dramatic development. On the other hand, source music may be and often *is* used as an *antithesis* to the dramatic action. We might find a hurdy-gurdy playing in a street scene involving a brutal killing or rape, where the source accompaniment could be more effective than conventional scoring.

COMPOSING TO DRAMATIC ACTION

Dramatic action in screenplays can be defined in many ways. We can have plot developments in dramatic sequences that do not describe physical action but rather set up tension that might call for increased movement in the music. We can also have dialog action such as arguments, hysteria, fright, disappointment, accidents, and many other emotional qualities. Physical action—struggles, belligerency, vehemence, fist fights, auto and foot chases—all indicate a different approach in the music construction.

Nonphysical action will usually be accompanied by dark orchestral colors, setting up tension and usually conceived with the use of low-register instruments. Great care must be taken in music construction in this area. In the case of arguments, the underlying approach should certainly be merely a fortification of the emotional strain and not an imitation of the tempo of the spoken dialog. At certain points it may be necessary to employ dramatic music accents, or reactions, as amplification to the existing tension being exhibited. In any event, the strength of the music in performing these accents, or reactions, has to be weighed very carefully. An effective device can be used many times with a volume increase in the orchestra and a subsequent accented dissonant chord supplying the necessary reaction without the addition of a heavier group of instruments which quite often could turn the intelligent dramatic music development into melodramatic or overtheatrical.

Consideration also has to be given to the effectiveness of dead silence, which *can* be more forceful than heavy orchestral sounds.

Hysteria must also be examined carefully. Whether the scene actually needs music or not is the prime question. If the actor or actress performing this emotion is of top quality, and the scene highly charged, the chances are that the performance alone will carry the scene very effectively. Music in this case could often detract from the dramatic action and thus defeat the desired effect. There is, of course, hysteria with little or no dialog. In this case music can be extremely valuable in describing the hidden or outward emotions of the performance. The strong tension that is possible to develop in the music can add greatly to the dramatic effect and, if constructed judiciously, can be of invaluable assistance.

Fright as an emotional reaction, not to be confused with hysteria, allows the composer to examine the *cause*, the *effect*, and the *result*. It further allows him to describe the fear that has been set up in the mind of the performer which many times will not fully be described by dialog. This psychological music probe can be extremely important in the dramatic development of such scenes. Take, for example, three characters in a story—the classic hero, heroine, and villain—with themes or motifs having been established for each. When the heroine is in a state of fright or shock caused primarily by an act of the villain, the use of the villain and heroine motifs can be written contrapuntally so as to supply a valid and effective polyphony, thus adding greatly to the dramatic impact. There are, of course, untold facets of the singular emotion of fright. The one to be depicted musically must be determined from the standpoint of what is going on *in the mind of the performer*.

The conventional music approach to struggles and chases has been the heavy, fast moving, sometimes hysterical orchestral sound. However, the more progressive composer will try to avoid this duplication of sound effects by music. Of course, the final decision as to how scenes such as these are to be handled, in the music application, many times rests with the producer. If he indicates that the particular scene needs ponderous heavy-handed music and the composer feels that this is unnecessary, it is then the composer's responsibility to convince the producer that a different plan could be more effective. It has been proved that in scoring a fist fight with only three percussion (drums) and two pianos, the overall result can be extremely effective. Further, with all of the recent advances in electronic instruments, it is very possible that the singular use of this medium could give a startling impression.

Fights and chases should not be an imitation of what we see and hear in the scene. Gang fights, body punches, running horses or cattle, foot chases—all have a sound within a certain range in the music scale: roughly, the range of the lower pitched instruments of the orchestra, and particularly in the drum, tympani, or percussion section. True, the upper, or higher sections of the orchestra are used extensively; but the great weight of the music will be felt in these low instruments. It would seem then that the hysteria generated by scenes such as these should be the prime consideration for intensification of this emotion. Energetic woodwinds and strings playing dissonant intervals in the middle and high registers, with occasional heavy punctuations by the brass, and percussion sections (not necessarily imitating the tempo of the action) can be most effective. An accented held note of high F above the staff by the entire violin section can give a reaction of practically equal dimension as could a full orchestral chord.

WRITING FUNCTIONAL (MOOD) MUSIC

The use of the word *mood* in describing the varied emotions set up in a photoplay is at the outset not only incorrect but a poor excuse for a more concise and proper description of the many passions and proclivities with which the word is associated.

Manvell and Huntley, in their book *The Technique of Film Music*, take issue with the use of another unfortunate term, "background music," which I present here (by permission of Focal Press, London):

> "*Background* music in relation to the film is a misleading term and, in any case, does not describe its function. *Integral* or *complementary* music might serve better, but the term *functional* is preferable, since the word implies the work a thing is designed to do. It is a proper and practical description of this newest branch of musical composition.
>
> "Functional music has a more complex relation to the action than realistic music since it is not an overt part of it. Here music *points*, underlines, links, emphasizes, or interprets the action, becoming part of the dramatic pattern of the film's structure."

With respect to writing *functional* music, we again quote Manvell and Huntley:

> "But functional music must, by its very nature and definition, perform some necessary part in building up various kinds of dramatic effect, and the general rule might seem to be that the greater the economy with which music is used the greater the dramatic effect it will achieve. This is, of course, a controversial point. The first consideration of both director and composer is, therefore, to decide where music *should not* just as much as where music *should* be introduced. Some directors have in mind the future presence of music on the soundtrack as they plan and shoot a particular sequence; others reach a decision as they supervise the editing of the film, sensing the need for musical support to carry and sustain the emotion of particular scenes and particular moments.
>
> "However a director discovers his need for music, the composer's own instinct in the matter should not be overlooked since, if he is a good composer of film music, he will know what his future score can achieve successfully at each point of the film where he is asked to assist. Once the passages are chosen and timed, he must go away and become a musician—actor, assuming the musical character of the film and creating music in the right dramatic mood for it."

With this basic psychology in mind, we must again refer to that thin line that separates music *assistance* from music *insistence*. In a romantic scene involving a man and a woman one must examine carefully where music assistance and insistence are indicated. Without the application of music, some scenes could be quite dull, particularly in the case of sparse dialog. Consequently, the music must seek out the inner emotion of these two people, determining whether it will build to a passionate climax, whether it will remain static, whether one or the other is not receptive, whether it is innocent, vibrant, sophisticated...

Particular attention must be given in the use of any romantic theme that might be designed for the two characters. It would certainly be grossly unwise to hear a full lush statement of this thematic material during any hesitancy in the development of the situation. If the scene builds to a climactic passionate embrace this also must be examined carefully. The conventional music approach is, of course, at this point, to hear the theme with all of the stops pulled out. In some cases this is perfectly acceptable, but not generally. What if the two people have given off collectively a building passion? If one is overpowering or reticent? If one is a case of rape? If one or the other is employing romantic tactics to achieve personal gain? All will indicate an entirely different approach. There is also the situation in which the two people exhibit shyness or innocence. The point of the final embrace, in this case, dictates the type of music approach—again, from the inner thinking rather than the outward display of the participants.

The great flexibility of the written music and the orchestral performance gives immense latitude in the music planning for such sequences. In the violin section alone, the dynamic possibilities are tremendous. In the case of strong romantic emotion, this section of instruments can play in unison or be heavily divided in the low, middle, or high register; as a counter melody to other instruments; a solo violin accompanied at times by the balance of the section. The group can perform delicately for hesitant romatic scenes. It can express subtle sophistication or innocence, and with the use of mutes it can convey excellent ethereal effects.

Examination should also be made in the use of the woodwind section (flutes, oboes, clarinets, and bassoons). The excessive or pointed use of any or all of the instruments in romantic sequences can be chancy. This group is not nearly as flexible as the string group. They, of course, will be able to speak loudly, moderately loudly, and softly; however, the individual color of the instrument remains constant. Unless used with caution, these instruments can become quite distracting, particularly in association with dialog.

The use of the brass section—trumpets and trombones—is equally precarious, especially when muted. The cup, straight, harmon, and buzzer mutes will immediately attract attention as a sound foreign to the intent of the scene. In this section the French horns are most valuable as an added color. They blend perfectly with almost any instrument or combination of instruments in the orchestra, even to the extent of taking some of the edge off the solo or collective instruments in the woodwind section.

This is not to imply that the brass or woodwind groups should never be used, but rather to suggest that these instruments should be used judiciously, with discretion. They are, of course, a very necessary addition to give the instrumental group the true orchestral sound or color.

General atmospheric music has in many instances been saddled with the term *neutral*. This probably refers to innocuous music used as "fill." Situations such as these sometimes indicate weaknesses in the plot development and they present great problems to the composer. With no definite advancement of the story line to guide him he will be faced with having to literally fill the gap with some music sounds in order to continue a sense of pace or tempo. It should not be distractingly melodic nor should it act as a sedative. One film composer terms this *nothing music*. Nevertheless, it is necessary; and without its application, scenes such as these could have a disastrous effect on the overall story. A feeling of movement in the writing is indicated under such circumstances; however, movement can be achieved in the writing without increasing the tempo or depending upon thematic development.

Intelligent chord progressions, changes of color (coupling of different instrumental combinations), the use of such melodic percussion instruments as the vibraphone, marimba, harp, piano, and harpsichord can give the feeling of movement an sustain the audience interest through periods such as these.

PRERECORDED MUSIC

A recent trend has been developing in which some film producers have been using music guide tracks composed of taped copies of existing phonograph records, in conjunction with the film editing process. They feel that a certain inspiration will be achieved by playing these tracks while cutting the film and following, roughly, the sense of the music to which they are listening. After the film has been edited, the composer, who has been assigned to write the final score, will attempt to create his individual and unique music for the scenes that were made at the cadence of the now-discarded guide tracks.

The dangers in this method of filmmaking are numerous. As related before, the incidents of the music for *The Graduate* and *2001—A Space Odyssey* shows us that unless duplication of the guide tracks is made, few producers will be satisfied with replacement music of original composition.

This method of music application is, however, not new. For many years some producers have been in the habit of previewing their films accompanied by music tracks salvaged from other earlier films. This music was intended to be temporary and was only used as a timesaving device to get the audience reaction with the possibility of the need for further editing before final scoring of the film. But producers can become so enamored with this temporary music that instructions would be given the composer, who would ultimately score the film, to duplicate, as much as possible, this temporary music.

This presents great problems to composers, not the least of which is the threat to an artist's personal integrity. And the composer who follows the dictum will find it virtually impossible to write music resembling the guide track closely enough to satisfy the producer. And, again: Some of the original music tracks may have been recorded with 70−80 musicians, whereas the composer of the new score, limited to perhaps half that number, will be expected to produce the same volume of sound that was contained in the original music.

At one time a certain Hollywood producer of very low budget films would avoid a music recording session and keep costs down with the following procedure. He would somehow acquire music tracks recorded for other films and have his film editor (he avoided the expense of a music editor) splice together and wind onto separate reels orchestral music that he classed as *romantic, dramatic, mysterioso, chases, fights*, etc. At the time of the dubbing or mixing of all of the sound tracks, his music reels would be threaded onto separate sound projectors and would be run simultaneously with the other sound tracks. The net result was that the music engineer at the control board would be able to project any of the music tracks merely by turning a dial. The producer would then instruct the engineer as to which scenes in the film would use what descriptive music. If he wanted dramatic music at a certain point, the engineer would turn up the gain on the amplifier with that type of music. My feeling was that this was a very poor and certainly unesthetic way to score a film. However, Quincy Jones had different thoughts:

> "I think that that's a better idea than just going into dubbing with the producer expecting what he has heard before or what he hears in his mind. At least it's *tangible*. You could say 'well,

that's a little old fashioned.' but you could at least pass judgment on it.

"With regard to this. I would like to go the opposite way so that the producer knows what's happening. That's why temporary tracks don't really bother me unless the producer falls in love with every line of music. I like to challenge the temporary track because producers may get pretty ambitious. Many times they will score that last reel with Stravinsky and he's a rough dude to follow—or even pretend to follow... Something that Stravinsky's worked on for years. and they load the whole last reel with it."

Musicians union contracts with the major producers forbid the use of any library or track music in the final release of a film. But even so, it would be possible to salvage from their music libraries the written music of these temporary tracks and simply record them again for the existing picture, thus complying with union regulations. This has been done innumerable times.

Referring again to the situation of the producer's use of guide tracks during the editing period, a point is brought up that seems quite valid. That is the possibility of composing and recording some or all of the dramatic music *before* photography. True, this presents technical problems, the most important of which could be limiting the freedom of editing to the length of the music for any given sequence. This could be overcome by designing the music flexibly enough to be lengthened or shortened or actually edited along with the cutting of the film. There is also the possibility that a postrecording session could be called for any corrections, extensions, or connecting links that might be needed following this editing period.

Misha Donet, in his article *Music in the Cinema* for the British publication *The Listener*, discusses dramatic music recorded prior to photography or editing.

"Perhaps the most fruitful approach to the positive use of music in the cinema. and towards greater understanding between director and composer. lies in a collaboration of the two artists before the shooting of the film begins. The most famous director—composer collaboration in the history of cinema is certainly that of Eisenstein and Prokofiev. who consistently planned the relationship between film and music. and the structural function of each. as part of the preparation of the shooting script. In *Alexander Nevsky*. for instance. several sequences were cut to the rhythm of Prokofiev's music. while in others the score was tailored to fit the tempo of the picture: in certain sections. a combination of both methods was used. The famous battle on ice in this film was almost balletic in conception, and one can only regret that Eisenstein and Prokofiev didn't take one further step and produce a genuine film ballet or opera. As it is, perhaps the nearest we have to true opera film is *Les Parapluies de Cherbourg* by Jacques Demy and Michel Legrand—an extremely original music film for which all the music was recorded in advance of the shooting, and of which the structure and rhythms were wholly determined by the early collaboration between director and composer.

Another interesting thought might be explored relative to dramatic music recorded prior to photography and then played on the set during the actual shooting. The argument against this: *What about the recording of the dialog?* The dialog could very easily be recorded later in synchronization with the filmed scene while being projected on a recording stage, or the playback machine on the set could simply be silenced during actual dialog.

Quincy Jones was questioned regarding his feeling about the theory of prerecording dramatic music. His answer:

"At one point, maybe a month before the final cut when you get the specific timings, the composer should be allowed to see the film in the rough-cut state—three to five times, maybe, depending on how quick he absorbs, and then do a preliminary scoring which would consist of attitudes, density, and character. It's almost like a display kit, in a sense, where you can have the chance of shooting a little extra music footage too, where the theme that the composer has in his mind can be presented in two or three different ways.

"Also, if there are a lot of chases they can feel out what they're after. No timing at all. Just generally using his own judgment of how much he will need for each sequence. Even if the recording session is done only to be thrown out later, they have a frame of reference when they sit down at those dumb music spotting sessions and say, start the music here and end it there. That, to me, is the biggest hassle in the world. How do they know what to start when they don't know what it's going to be? And when a director says *start the music there*, he in his mind hears something. He's going to associate with something that he's heard before. He *has* to because he doesn't hear a new sound there. For instance, many times I would like to start a cue where it evolves itself from some natural sound effect that has a shape or contour of a tonality, and you start to sneak in the music. It could be an atonal kind of haze with strings that just hang, and you're not even aware of, and it starts to grow and grow and where the producer said *start the music*, okay, just continue it in more musical sense."

David Grusin was also questioned about the same subject:

Q. Was the scoring for *Midnight Cowboy* similar to the application of music to *The Graduate*?

A. Yes, I think so. John Barry wrote a few things as well as myself, but it was mostly a supervisory job.

Q. Did they cut the film to the music taken from the discs?

A. I don't know. I suspect that they did so for a few sequences.

Q. Why isn't it possible to write and record the music score before photography?

A. I think Norman Jewison tried it in *The Thomas Crown Affair*. I think Michel Legrand recorded one session. Then a few sequences were edited to the music tracks; however, they were rerecorded after that. I don't know why it wouldn't work.

Music is a prime ingredient in virtually every film or videotape production. And where a particular production's budget won't allow assemblage of musicians and the services of a composer, the logical and economical alternative is the use of canned music from a production music library. And wasteful as it may seem, music written for a specific production must stay with that production—it does not find its way to a canned-music library. Musicians-union rules forbid the reuse of contract music regardless of how applicable that music may be to another project.

This rule applies also to television feature films.

To satisfactorily score scenes with library music it may at times be necessary to use many different portions from one or more prerecorded cues. Rarely will the character of the prerecorded music follow the dramatic reactions, changes of spirit, or tempo that requires music accompaniment.

Special difficulties may be encountered in application of canned music to film-story openings (main titles) and closings (end titles). Since these are photographed before music selection, it would be pure chance to find lengths of music that match the photographic footage. In cases such as this, if the production is of enough importance, the production music service can subcontract the composition and recording of not only opening and closing themes but thematic variations to generally cover different emotions and dramatic characterizations that might be encountered throughout the project.

Production music is generally of very high quality and normally employs large complements of musicians and skilled film composers. This becomes very attractive to producers of low-budget films.

In 1972 **Capitol Music Service** commissioned a score for an American film, to be written and recorded in Japan. Since this was Capitol's first such foreign venture, an audition performance of the music material was arranged for final approval. The orchestra played the music in Japan and the sound was received in Hollywood via satellite. This, coupled with a three-way telephone hookup, enabled changes to be made on the spot, and thus saved a considerable amount of time.

THE CLICK TRACK

When dense, emulsion-coated film passes through the sound portion of the projector it produces silence. When the emulsion is removed, light passes through the clear spot and triggers a noise generator. The removal of emulsion by simply scratching it clean in minute areas, at intervals, will produce pops or clicks. Although many music recording studios are now equipped with electronic metronome devices that produce clicks in various speeds or tempos, it is well that a close examination be made of the preparation of the click loop or track.

The click track enables the composer, when he is involved with a sequence in which there are many time-dependent music reactions or cues, to write his music to the tempo of the clicks which he has predetermined.

If a scene is one long continuous battle and he wishes to emphasize many points during the sequence, the composer will decide in which tempo the music is to be played. Following this, he will instruct the music editor to construct a click loop (a continuous loop of appropriately nicked film) or click track.

The composer will make his decision as to tempo with the aid of the metronome and a conversion chart which will give him the equivalent spacing of frames, between clicks, to metronome beats. (See Table 4-1.) A metronome beat of 120 will mean that a click or pop will occur on every twelfth frame.

Much time and research has been spent by authors, notably Earle Hagen (*Scoring for Films*) and the late Robert Emmet Dolan (*Music in Modern Media*) in explaining the technical aspects of constructing the click track. In Mr. Hagen's opening paragraph he explains that he has worked out a mathematical formula with which any piece of music can

Table 4-1. Metronome Click Conversion Chart.

CLICKS PER MINUTE	NICKED FRAME	SPROCKET HOLE	CLICKS PER MINUTE	NICKED FRAME	SPROCKET HOLE
60	24th		112	12th	3rd
63	22nd	3rd	116	12th	1st
66	21st	3rd	120	12th	
69	20th	3rd	126	11th	2nd
72	20th		132	10th	3rd
76	18th	3rd	138	10th	2nd
80	18th		144	10th	
84	17th	1st	152	9th	2nd
88	16th	1st	160	9th	
92	15th	3rd	168	8th	2nd
96	15th		176	8th	1st
100	14th	1st	184	7th	3rd
104	13th	3rd	192	7th	2nd
108	13th	1st			

accent any given point in a sequence to within 2½ milliseconds with the aid of a properly prepared click track.

Although Mr. Dolan does not go into the higher mathematics of click preparation he does offer a further means of assistance through the click track process. He suggests that in certain cases the use of the strong click on the downbeat of the bar (the first beat) with the following clicks in the bar of less intensity. This is accomplished by simply removing the film emulsion in greater quantity on these beats than the following beats in the bar.

The music editor, following the completion of the click track, will then make up a music cue sheet indicating all action, dialog, etc. according to the clicks (see Fig. 4-1).

Following the delivery of the music cue sheet, the composer will construct his music for the sequence—not to timing, but to the consecutively numbered clicks (see Fig. 4-2).

The click track provides insurance that music punctuations and effects will fall perfectly into place. In fact, when the conductor is faced with an extremely tight budget he may score an entire film with the aid of the click track.

In the case of romantic, dramatic, or any such scenes that would indicate more freedom of expression than the rigid

```
                        MUSIC CUE SHEET
                        PRODUCTION 1102
                  REEL 5 PART 4 - REEL 6 PART 1
                      12 FRAME CLICK LOOP

CLICK
  1     START ON CUT OF PEOPLE RUNNING TOWARD JAIL

  4     CUT TO INTERIOR OF JAIL - VEGA REACTS AND TURNS
        FAST - TAKES CHAINS AND DRAGS PRISONERS TOWARD
        STAIRS

19½    CUT TO EXTERIOR - CROWD RUNNING - VARIOUS SHOTS

 39     CUT TO VEGA AT BOTTOM OF STAIRS - IN OFFICE

 43     O.S. "VEGA!" - HE STOPS - REACTS

44½    CUT TO CROWD RUNNING TO JAIL - THROWING ROCKS

 48     ROCK HITS WINDOW

 55     VEGA BOLTS DOOR

 58     "LET'S GET THE HELL OUT OF HERE" AS HE DRAGS AT
        MEN - THEY YELL AT EACH OTHER

 74     END DIALOG

 79     CUT TO EXTERIOR - ESTEVEZ AND CROWD ARRIVE AT
        DOOR OF JAIL

 97     VEGA AND PRISONERS OUT OF WINDOW - BACK OF JAIL -
        TELLS THEM TO GET INTO TRUCK

110     CUT TO ESTEVEZ YELLING "BRING THEM OUT, VEGA!"

117     CUT TO PRISONERS IN TRUCK - VEGA HEADS FOR
        DRIVER'S SEAT - GETS IN

129     TURNS STARTER SWITCH

132     CUT BACK TO CROWD YELLING AT DOOR

143     START TO BREAK DOWN DOOR

143½   BACK TO TRUCK - PRISONERS REACT TO STARTER NOT
        WORKING

152     BACK TO CROWD RAMMING DOOR

155     BACK TO STARTER SWITCH

158     BACK TO CROWD RAMMING DOOR

160     BACK TO SWITCH - PAN UP TO VEGA

165     TRUCK MOTOR STARTS

168     BACK TO CROWD

172     BREAK DOWN DOOR - ENTER JAIL

177     BACK TO TRUCK MOVING OUT

189½   CUT TO EXTERIOR OF JAIL - CROWD RUSHING OUT

191     "THEY'RE NOT HERE" - SEE TRUCK MOVING IN DISTANCE

199     "THERE THEY GO"

202     FAST PAN TO TRUCK

202½   CUT TO VEGA DRIVING - HE REACTS TO MAN RUNNING
        TOWARD TRUCK

204     CUT TO MAN RUNNING

207     TRUCK HITS MAN

209     MAN HITS STREET

209½   CROSS OVER TO NEXT CUE
```

Fig. 4-1. The click track can make the music cue sheet extremely precise.

Fig. 4-2. From the cue sheet's click-track information, the composer can construct his music for the sequences.

tempo of the click loop would allow, composers will write *against* the clicks, avoiding as much as possible any feeling of one set tempo.

In a $^4/_4$ bar there usually is a slight sense of emphasis on the downbeat. This can be avoided in the writing by spacing the structure so that the melodic or harmonic progressions fall unevenly, thus according a sense of relaxation of the strict metronomic beat. This can also be accomplished by interspersing $^3/_4$, $^2/_4$, or $^5/_4$ bars.

With involved, fast-moving chase or fight music it will not be unusual for every member of the orchestra to wear a headset to hear the click tempo along with the conductor. More often, however, headsets may be worn by the percussion group and possibly members of the brass section.

David Grusin, when asked if he made use of click tracks or loops as a timesaving device, said that he did not:

> "I make use of the click track to try to hold the band together in a spread-out situation, where they can't hear the rhythm section.... Once in a while, when a sequence is really "cuey," I will use it so that the music will fall in place at certain checkpoints; but mostly it is just to keep the orchestra together. This could be solved, incidentally, if everybody in the band could wear headsets and hear everybody else. It would be ideal. Or if they could just hear the rhythm section. In some of the newer studios they are patching things together and playing it back through the headsets."

Alex North says he does use the click track as a timesaver:

> "Again, it depends on the kind of scene it is. Not *necessarily* for timesaving but for a split-second moment when you have to accept something right on the nose, like in a chase or a battle. In most scenes I prefer using just free timing so that the music can breathe, and there is room for ritards and accelerandos, but I'm not against the use of click tracks."

Variable Click Track

The *variable* click track is normally used only with sequences such as marching bands, parades, ballroom or nightclub dancing, and other such scenes that need music of a set tempo.

Unfortunately, many times sequences such as these will have been photographed without the aid of a temporary tempo guide track; consequently, the edited version of these scenes may come to the composer and conductor with variations in tempo. It is then necessary to have a variable click track made so that these changes of tempo, hopefully slight, can be matched during the orchestra recording.

Intercuts can create problems that necessitate a variable click track. Consider scenes involving a marching brass band containing intercuts of various angles of the band, cuts to marchers, spectators, baton twirlers, the bandleader, etc. Or scenes of customers dancing in a nightclub or ballroom, with cuts away from the dancing to dialog scenes, and then back to the dancing (where the dance music continues under the dialog). Extended concert, ballet, opera, or symphony music scenes will demand cuts away from the performers at times to the audience, if only to relieve any static feeling that such a lengthy single exposure might give off. These and any other sequences that will need the application of rhythmic music need as much assistance as possible from the film editor.

If the scenes have not been photographed with playback, the film editor (and music editor) must *preserve the tempo* as much as possible, particularly when cutting back to the music performers. It is all too easy to have a band marching left, right, left, right, and then cut back to them marching right, left, right, left.

With judicious editing, this can be corrected by deleting or adding a few frames of film. This does not fully erase the problem of the music conductor having to use a click track, but it does assist in smoother, less distracting transitions.

The ideal method to avoid the necessity of using the variable click track during postrecording is to determine the tempo before shooting and have available a click loop (continuous film loop appropriately marked with tempo clicks) to be played on the set during the take. This is not always possible, as in the case of marching bands, rodeos, and other outdoor scenes that involve visual music but are too extensive in scope to employ audible click loops. However, it must be emphasized that whenever the director is involved with more intimate visual music he should not ignore the use of the click loop. The advantage of this procedure is obvious: at the final recording it will be a simple matter to match the tempo with that of the same click loop used during photography.

Integrating
the Music Score

The film production continuity chart, Fig. 5-1, lists two types of motion pictures. One includes specialty music sequences and the other consists of feature films that do not contain music specialties.

Music *specialty* means visual display, on the screen, of solo or group singing, dancing, instrumentals, and any other exhibitive entertainment of a musical nature that may be inserted into the dramatic development as an integrated part of the film.

PRERECORDING

When the film is a musical or any other film that requires on-screen musical performances, the first order of business is selection of those performers. These decisions are normally made during casting. In the area of vocal soloists, a leading actor or actress may be designated as the performer. If he or she is not a singer, a professional vocalist will be hired to perform the music during the prerecording, or recording of music prior to photography (to be used during the shooting sessions for syncing the music with the visual action). The technical and precise synchronization of the picture and prerecorded music is effected by the music editor later.

Vocal Soloists

The material to be recorded may be (1) an existing copyrighted piece of music, (2) newly written for the

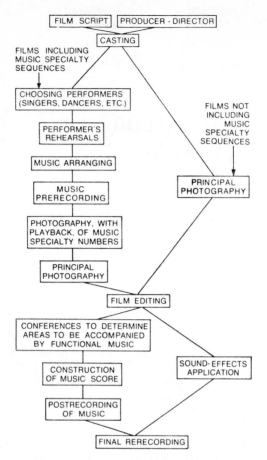

Fig. 5-1. Functional diagram, motion picture production.

production, (3) adapted from the main dramatic theme, or (4) music in the public domain (not protected by copyright).

If a copyrighted song or piece of music is considered for use, a license for the use of this music must be obtained from the copyright holder. The producer can either make these arrangements directly with the music publisher or negotiate through one of the copyright service organizations such as the *American Mechanical Rights Association*, the *Copyright Service Bureau, Ltd.*, or *Harry Fox Agency, Inc.*

The advantage in dealing through associations such as these is that it relieves prolonged negotiations with the copyright owners. A simple inquiry to the agency requesting a quotation for the use of the copyrighted music usually brings prompt response. Such information as type and extent of use as well as film title should be included in the inquiry.

Another important function of these agencies is that they maintain extensive files regarding the *public domain* status of a great many compositions.

Where the music is to be performed on-screen, newly written songs will generally be the work of professional songwriters whose agreement will grant exclusive film performance rights to the producer. This will also be the case in the development of the composer's main theme as a song. Music in the public domain presents no license problems and may be used at will. Attention should be given here to the fact that published *arrangements* of music—including public domain music—*are* copyrighted; even though the basic music may be used without license fee, the arrangements of that music may not.

The vocal soloist may or may not possess an orchestral arrangement of the music to be performed. If he has an existing arrangement, this should be turned over to the conductor to be examined for suitability and possible elaboration to fit into the plan for the balance of the music in the film. Too many vocal and instrumental soloists as well as solo dancers will have nightclub or stage-performance arrangements that, while suitable for smaller groups, may not be applicable for use in the film production. If the performer does not have an arrangement, an arranger will be hired to tailor the music according to the producer's requirements. The arranger may work directly with the vocalist in planning the music sequence.

When one of the film actors is to appear to be performing a number in a picture, and a dubbed-in voice is required, some complications set in. Usually, this means that a variety of talented professionals will be auditioned to allow selection of a voice that most closely matches that of the film star. In cases such as these, the conductor and arranger—and often the director and choreographer—will work on the plan for presentation of the song. Most important will be the length of the final footage of this music—film sequence. The timing of this number has to be worked out carefully to insure a good tight fit into the overall length of the film.

After determining the most comfortable key for the *dub-in* vocalist as well as the size and type of orchestra that will be used, the arranger will be in a position to complete the transcription.

Specialty Dance Sequences

Dance numbers require the addition of two more members to the team—the *choreographer* and the *rehearsal pianist*; these two work together in laying out the musical routines. The pianist should be able to write music because he will be expected to present an intelligent music outline to the arranger following the rehearsal period. The music to be used for these routines can either be variations of songs used in the film or music designed specifically for the dance. As to the latter, the choreographer, as dance director, may wish to work with both the rehearsal pianist and the arranger because of the arranger's unique expertise in adaptation of musical numbers. In some films, of course, the composer of the final score may create the music for the routines in association with the choreographer.

Vocal Groups

It is customary with extensive choral singing to assign a specialist choral conductor/arranger who usually will choose and hire the singers. He will normally not be involved with the orchestral arrangement but rather the arranging for only the voices. He may or may not be one of the singers. If the group singing is in conjunction with a vocal soloist, the soloist's voice coach or arranger will be involved in the overall planning. And if the vocalists, either soloist or group, are to be used with dancing sequences, the orchestra arranger must be included as well as the dance director, particularly if the singers are to be photographed.

Instrumental Soloists or Groups

The complications with instrumentalists are slight. True, the same problems arise in choosing the music to be performed; but on the whole the planning is simplifier to some extent.

The instrumental group may or may not be accompanied by orchestra. As in the case of the vocal soloist, the background orchestral arrangement should be turned over to the conductor for examination.

Low-Budget Alternatives

In low-budget films many shortcuts can be used. It is entirely possible that a composer may assume all or a great part of the responsibilities in prerecording planning and execution. Orchestral arranging, vocal arranging and conducting, securing music licenses, music supervision—all are sometimes the complete domain of a single individual. Further, the prerecording may be bypassed altogether by recording the music to accompany vocal and dancing sequences with a temporary piano track. In the case of vocalists, this is accomplished with the use of a soundproof isolation booth for the singer. Headsets are worn by the musicians so they can hear the vocalist indirectly. Since the vocalist will appear on one tape track while the piano or other musical instruments appear on another, the piano track may be discarded later and replaced by an orchestral accompaniment in the *postrecording* period.

Temporary music to accompany dancing is a little more involved. Here, the music should follow as closely as possible the planned future orchestral arrangement, because tempos and changes of tempo will be of importance during photography.

The Prerecording Session

The physical prerecording is where the emphasis will be on technical perfection. This music, which will be of prime importance and demand undivided audience attention, should be letter perfect.

The prerecording session is done on the recording stage with considerably more time usually taken in order to perfect the individual pieces of music. All of the people associated with the planning are expected to be in attendance. In addition to the soloists, these would include arrangers (in large-scale, high-budget musicals, more than one arranger will likely be assigned), vocal coaches, music editor, copyist, and choreographer. And very often the producer/director will attend.

Technically, the vocal and orchestra entities will be recorded on separate tape tracks and will make use of the isolation booth. When the composite track—vocal and orchestra tracks blended into one unit—is prepared for use on the set, the voice or voices will usually be recorded on the composite at a higher level than normal. This is so that the vocalist can concentrate on matching the voice line without accompaniment distraction. If the prerecording is of a piece of music consisting of variations in tempo, pauses, individual stylizations, or other portions of the music where the voice entrances may not be in strict rhythm, it may be necessary for the music editor to apply warning pops or clicks in these areas so that photographic synchronization will be less difficult. To clarify, if in a song a note is sustained for longer than normal time the performer will hear, on the playback, two or three distinct pops or clicks preceding the start of the next phrase.

Having separate tracks for music and vocals offers a couple of fallout advantages, too. The vocalist may be dissatisfied with his performance and wish to record his singing at a later time by listening to the existing orchestra track through a headset. Also, the producer may be dissatisfied with the singer's voice quality and wish to replace the track with a different vocalist.

In present-day recording practice, it is not unusual to employ as many as 24 tracks in orchestral recording. This allows for quality control in dubbing. (An off-key instrument can be deleted if it has been recorded on a separate tape track.)

Production numbers of any great length will usually be recorded in sections which, after shooting, will be edited together. Music introductions and transitions will be added at the postrecording session.

The mechanics of prerecording are fairly well cut and dried: with a vocal number, the tone or pitch of the beginning of the song will be struck on either the piano or orchestra bells followed by an audible count, in tempo, by the conductor—one, two, three, four, *downbeat*. This count is very important because only in this way, during photography, will the performer know when to start the song. Of course, these preparatory counts and tones will be cut off and discarded after the scene is shot.

In the area of prerecording *source* music, certain points should be brought out. Using as an example dance music recorded for ultimate photography which will use an on-scene orchestra, the tempo of the music must first be decided. Also, the decision as to the size of the orchestra to be photographed should be made. Some latitude is acceptable with respect to differences in the size of the recording orchestra compared to the group that will be photographed. Still, it would be ludicrous to record music with 30 or 35 musicians, though showing only six or eight on the scene. This on-scene orchestra will not be made up of the same musicians that made the original recording. The performers that will be photographed are called sideline musicians. Because the union scale for sidelining is considerably lower than that for film recording, sideline calls rarely attract recording musicians. The sideline orchestra is comprised of people who *do* read music, however, and usually quite capably.

The written music for the recording is preserved and, during photography, will be used by this sideline group to insure realism. These orchestra performers simply mimic the music that is heard from the playback.

Following the prerecording, the songs will be copied from the original tracks for the singer's use in rehearsal prior to photographing the scenes. Every attempt is made to allow as much time as possible between prerecording and shooting so the performer may thoroughly familiarize himself with the music.

SHOOTING TO PLAYBACK

The term playback means either prerecorded music that is played on the set during photography or the playing of music following the recording for purposes of review.

The playback that is to be used during photography will be a copy of the original recording.

Most directors favor the use of discs in this operation because of the simplicity in marking the record with a grease pencil at the various starting points. The playback machine is, of course, interlocked with the camera so that no synchronization deviation can occur.

In photographing vocal scenes, lip sync (mouthing to the playback) is of vital importance. In complicated production numbers it may be necessary for more than one person to supervise this all-important phase. The responsibility of

111

deciding whether the take is acceptable or should be done over rests entirely with these people. They will concentrate on lip movements of the performer from the closest possible vantage point, and the slightest deviation from the playback will mean rejection of the take.

Al Jolson's voice was used for all of the playbacks in *The Jolson Story*. Larry Parks, as Jolson in the film, was to "perform" these songs. In order to assure the utmost realism during photography, the volume of the playback machine was raised to an extremely high level so that Parks could literally belt the music and not be heard over the very loud sound of the playback. Thus, perfect realism was achieved.

When shooting a scene that involves dialog during playback, the machine is silenced during the dialog but continues to run silently so that following the dialog the music can be heard in proper sequence.

Tempo must be preserved when dancing is shown in dialog scenes even with the music turned off. Various methods are used, such as continuing the tempo with a cadence of lights blinking off-camera or with small radio receivers worn inconspicuously by the dancers so that they may hear the music out of microphone range. This method of playback is very desirable in sequences where the dancers will be singing.

In some involved scenes it is possible that the sound of the playback through the speakers on the set will be continued during dialog. In this case the actors, at some future date, will rerecord the dialog while viewing the scenes via projection on a recording stage. The trade term for this procedure is *looping*. Looping is quite common with exterior dialog scenes during which sound interference such as wind, aircraft, traffic, etc. is present and cannot be controlled.

Direct recording (on the set) is at times necessary when either a greater freedom of expression can be achieved in spontaneous performance or the expense and time involved with playback recording, set equipment, and personnel are beyond the budget limits. If at all possible, this type of recording should be limited to as small a group of accompanying musicians as feasible. The sound stage, or set, is not designed acoustically for music recording; therefore, the results may leave much to be desired. Music recorded on the set with other than solo proportions will rarely balance with final postrecorded music recorded in professional studios or sound stages. A singer may accompany himself on a silent piano while a professional pianist provides actual accompaniment out of camera range. Such techniques prove workable where the music accompaniment is minimal.

POSTRECORDING

To describe this function, and with the attempt to avoid technical language as much as possible, let us follow through an average film music recording period from the beginning.

The composer has completed his score, which is now going through the copying process. The contractor will be notified as to the instrumentation that will be needed, and the musicians will be advised as to the date of the recording. These musicians will not comprise a set, organized orchestra; although many have played together under the baton of different conductors, they are chiefly free-lance musicians.

In his construction of the music, it is highly unlikely that the composer will have written the entire score for the full complement of musicians to be employed for the recording. Let us assume that the largest group that the composer has written for is 63 players. In the process of creating the score he will write various sequences for smaller groups—possibly different combinations of instruments that can be salvaged from the maximum orchestra. It now becomes a matter of mathematics, in the interest of economy, to plan the recording session so that, if possible, no musicians will be idle, for which time they will have to be paid. Let us further assume that the length of the entire score will be 55 minutes, of which only 30 minutes will be written for the full complement, 18 minutes for approximately half of the group, and the balance of 15 minutes for an entirely different combination of exotic instruments that are not a part of the existing group.

The composer will first attempt to calculate how much music he will be able to record per hour. He is fully aware that the minimum recording session, by union regulations, is three hours, beyond which the musicians will be paid on a quarter-hour basis. He is also aware that during each hour of recording a rest period of ten minutes must be granted to the players. Consequently, if he feels that he will be able to record five minutes of actual music playing time each hour, he will then be faced with a schedule that requires 6 hours of recording for the 30 minutes in which he will be using the large orchestra.

When the 30 minutes of music has been recorded, those musicians who will not participate further in the film will be dismissed and the session continued with those remaining.

Musicians go on being employed using this strategy—larger groups are recorded first to avoid costly idle periods, and then they are released as soon as possible so that available recording time can be used as economically as possible.

With all of this arithmetic out of the way, the music recording engineer will be notified as to the instrumentation that will be used. He will then plan the setup of the orchestra—seating arrangements, microphone placement, arranging of baffles and other mechanical aids that he may think necessary. If any unusual music effects are planned, the composer may wish to discuss these personally with the engineer prior to the day of recording so that less time will be consumed during the session.

In planning identification cue numbers for music to be postrecorded, any prerecordings that have been made must be taken into consideration. For example, the third reel may have as its first cue *dramatic music* (to be postrecorded), following which may be a prerecorded production number such as a dance, vocal, etc. Further along in the reel dramatic music may be planned. The identifying numbers would then be M-3 Part 1 (or M-3-1) for the first dramatic music, M-3-2 for the prerecording, and M-3-3 for the following functional music. In other words, all music must appear in sequence, despite the fact that it may not have been recorded in the proper order.

If any cues are to be recorded with projection of scenes on the screen, the music editor will prepare the film sequence on separate reels with proper cue numbers as identification. He will also have prepared any click loops or tracks that may be needed during the recording.

The Postrecording Session

On the day of the recording the musicians will probably arrive well ahead of the starting time. The percussionists need time to set up their instruments, and the rest of the orchestra will need time to warm up and make sure their instruments are in tune. Heavier instruments—such as harp, tympani, drums and accessories. Novachord, Hammond or Yamaha organ—and others that are not available in the studio will have been delivered by truck.

Placement of the instruments will vary with different studios because it will be dependent upon the acoustic properties of the stage. Recording technicians have found the proper groupings in a given studio to achieve the best possible result. Microphones will be scattered throughout the orchestra normally beamed to the strings, the bass, trumpets and trombones. horns, possibly more than one on the woodwind, piano, celeste, harp, guitar(s), percussion, and any unusual instruments. Several *overall* microphones will be used to add perspective to the close pickups of the individual instruments.

In attendance at the recording will be the copyist, contractor, music editor, orchestrator, arranger, choreographer (at prerecordings), vocalists and vocal conductor, and usually the producer or director.

In the soundproof booth, occupied by the recording engineer and his elaborate control board, will be the recording console with an operator. Figures 5-2 and 5-3 show,

Fig. 5-2. The Glen Glenn music scoring stage at Paramount Studios in Hollywood.

115

Fig. 5-3. The control booth and panel at Paramount's Glen Glenn studio.

respectively, a music scoring stage and control booth at the Glen Glenn soundstage at Paramount Studios.

Most major film operations use only 35 mm sprocket-driven magnetic tape for music master tracks. This insures perfect synchronization; however, many times conventional audio tape (sans sprockets) will be used in conjunction with sync pulses applied at the time of the recording. Sync pulses are formed from a supersonic tone, and are used to control the speed of any tape machine equipped to receive these pulses.

Included in the furnishings of the booth will be a desk and chair usually occupied by the orchestrator or arranger who may at times make suggestions to the conductor regarding orchestra balance or convey to the engineer the plan and intent of the music.

We have now arrived at the starting time. The conductor, on his raised podium, signals the oboe to sound the note A, to which the orchestra will tune as a unit. Following this, the conductor announces the cue number of the first piece of music to be recorded, and the rehearsal of this music begins. During this rehearsal, which may take considerable time in order for the musicians to familiarize themselves with the individual composer, the engineer will be in the process of balancing the orchestra, recording portions of the rehearsal as a test.

After any written errors in the music have been corrected, microphones have been moved to more strategic positions, and the conductor, engineer, and orchestrator are satisfied with the performance, a take will be attempted. This is always preceded with a voice slate—an announcement as to production, cue, and take number. This is the means by which any recorded sequence may be later identified.

The conductor may or may not request a playback of the recorded sequence. With low-budget films, the conductor will usually listen to the playback of at least the first cue in order to assure himself of a satisfactory overall balance.

In certain cases two or more different recordings may be made for the same sequence with the intention of playing and rerecording them simultaneously in the subsequent dubbing process. In a scored battle scene during which a bugler rides by, the evident presence of the bugler necessitates a close perspective. So the orchestra is recorded at one time, the bugler at another; a later dubbing operation allows the tracks to be integrated. The same is true with any solo instruments that may be performing *source* music against a backdrop of functional dramatic music.

MUSIC EDITING

Following the recording, all of the preferred takes will be transferred to 35 mm sprocket-driven magnetic tape for delivery to the music editor's cutting room. The master music tracks are retained at the recording studio so that reprints (duplicates of tracks) may be made if ordered by the music editor.

Music editing or *cutting* involves less actual editing than preparation for recording and dubbing. Rarely will the editor revise, interpolate, add, or delete parts of the score.

The normal music editing procedure following postrecording will start with the editor's receipt of the rolls of transferred music from the recording studio. The editor separates the music cues from the 35 mm reels that contain the recordings, and plays them back while viewing the appropriate film footage on his Moviola. With music having been recorded to timing, it is rare that video and audio will stay in perfect synchronization. The music editor effectively moves the music track forward or backward, as necessary, to compensate for asynchronous portions.

The basic music track will be labeled **Music 1**. In the event that a cue will finish with a second cue overlapping the first, a second track is labeled **Music 2**. With involved overlays, or music playing at the same time on different tracks, the music editor can be involved with many labeled tracks, all of which have to be prepared from the basic start mark with the application of blank film leader to cover the silence preceding the entrance and following the finish.

During this assembly process he will be constructing a dubbing log sheet with exact footages (not timings) from the beginning to the finish of each music cue. These footages will be marked on the log sheet in chronological order from zero to the end of the last piece of music contained in the reel. (See Fig. 5-4.)

In the log sheet of Fig. 5-4 the editor is using three tracks which will be projected simultaneously during the dubbing session. (The reason for three tracks is that at one point there exists the functional orchestra scoring along with separate tracks for a roll on the cymbal and tympani beats.) The diagonal lines between the numerals indicate the exact length of the music in terms of film footage. Lines are only roughly proportional to footage, since the beginning and end of each line are marked with actual footage indications. Hence, M-100 starts at the 12 ft mark and finishes at 65 ft.

Notice that 9 ft from the beginning of the reel, there is indicated the word *pop*. This is a visual punched-hole flash and an audible pop, which is necessary for synchronization purposes when the film eventually reaches the negative cutter. Every reel must include this tone at the 9 ft point.

The first music cue begins at 12 ft and, as the line indicates, will finish at 65 ft. At 63 ft we find a second music cue starting (on music track 2) and underlapping the first with the indication *sneak*. This tells the engineer to start the music softly and increase the volume (the crescendo mark) to the level of the outgoing track. At 91 ft the roll on the cymbal appears on music track 1; and at 92 ft the tympani beats on track 3. The engineer will have three tape tracks running from 91 to 108 ft and two tracks continuing to 156 ft. Here we find

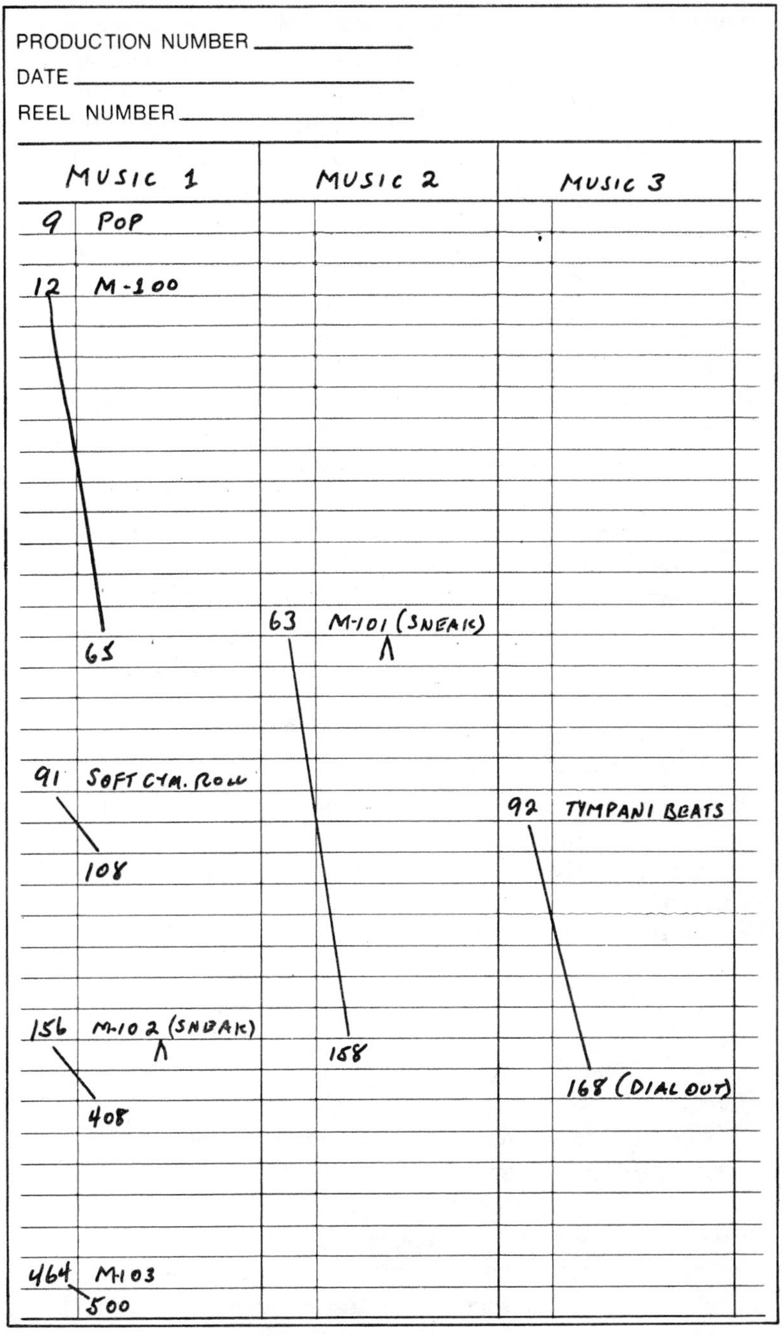
PRODUCTION NUMBER ____________
DATE ____________
REEL NUMBER ____________

MUSIC 1		MUSIC 2		MUSIC 3	
9	POP				
12	M-100				
	65	63	M-101 (SNEAK)		
91	SOFT CYM. ROLL			92	TYMPANI BEATS
	108				
156	M-102 (SNEAK)		158		
					168 (DIAL OUT)
	408				
464	M-103				
	500				

Fig. 5-4. Dubbing log sheet.

music cue M-102, on track 1, underlapping (*sneak* again) the finish of M-101 on track 2. The tympani beats continue on track 3 to 168 ft, where the engineer is instructed to dial out the track, it being apparently overlength. M-102 finishes at 408 ft with M-103 (on track 1) playing from 464 to 500 ft without complications.

RERECORDING

Dubbing or *Mixing* is the bringing together onto a single master all of the music tracks that are to be presented simultaneously. The process of dubbing or mixing is often called *rerecording*, particularly when it refers to combining all of the component sounds—dialog, sound effects, and music. The rerecording operations are done while viewing the projected film on a screen. All of this will be under the control of usually three expert sound engineers, one of which will be handling dialog, one controlling sound effects, and the other to deal with music.

The rerecording studio is typically quite large, with a massive control console at one end and a panoramic projection screen at the other end. Adjacent to the screen will be an illuminated footage counter to indicate the running footage of the film during projection. All dubbing is calculated to footage lengths and not timing.

A soundproof area adjacent to the stage will house perhaps a dozen or more 35 mm playback-only sound projectors, which feed into the dubbing console. Each of these playback machines will reproduce a separate sound track; one or more for dialog, two or more for music, and as many others as required for sound effects.

Sound effects become the real problem. Isolated sound effects may have been recorded on the dialog track at the time of shooting—doors opening and closing, doorbells and telephones ringing, running or walking footfalls, automobiles starting or running by, and many others. A great majority of these might need to be replaced in order to convey a heightened degree of realism. These replacements will then be incorporated onto the sound-effect tracks. Added to this could be battle scenes which will need many tracks running simultaneously in order to give the proper effect—overlapplng gunshots, yelling, bullet ricochets and other sounds of battle.

The dubbed or mixed sound is recorded onto a single magnetic tape which later will be technically rerecorded onto the optical track that occupies one edge of the release print.

Films of indoor sequences are very often dubbed with *room noise*, an almost inaudible hiss that is said to enhance realism. When this is sometimes omitted, it can create a disturbing uneasiness while viewing the film because of the unlifelike complete silence.

Relating the Score to the Story

It doesn't take an accomplished musician or conductor to know that the music accompanying a filmed segment has to reflect the mood (or establish it) represented by the scene or action being depicted. But scoring involves more than merely mood-matching, for the music should be capable of standing up alone as an integrated whole. It need not have a beginning, a middle, and an end—indeed, many music segments are far too short to possess a complete body; but it must be whole, and it must be *listenable*. In analyzing a score, we speak in terms of heaviness, thinness, strength and fullness, appropriateness of tempo. It is important to understand these and other such terms as well as their significance before making an attempt to analyze a score or determine the requirements for one, because these are the qualities that combine to make up the whole.

BASIC ANALYSIS

When we examine a score, it helps to have some sort of yardstick for gaging its suitability or appropriateness. But music is a subjective thing that defies grading and classification, and so it is unlikely that any two people will agree entirely when it comes to selection of music for filmed sequences. Still, there are certain common, clearly definable

Fig. 6-1. Orchestrated score sheet for analysis. Note distinguishing characteristic of trumpet line.

elements of any musical passage that can be considered in determining applicability: these include a comparison of the music tempo to the implied tempo of the portrayed scene, noticing the number of notes that are written in each bar, assessing the character of solo instruments as well as the feeling of the solo passages, etc.

In the orchestrated score of Fig. 6-1 we observe several points: The tempo is moderately fast—2½ seconds per bar (:02½). The trumpets are playing in high register. The tympani plays a considerable number of notes along with the piano, which itself plays strong chords. Without even analysis, a brief glance tells us this music is heavy and strong and moves at a fairly rapid pace.

To detect the most prominent part of the music, we look for notes that do not seem to follow the pattern established by the ensemble as a whole—in this case, the trumpets. The trumpets, then, indicate the motif that is of prime importance.

In the two score sheets of Fig. 6-2 we find a different situation. Starting with the last half of bar 2 we observe the entrance of two Spanish (nonamplified) guitars, one of which is marked SOLO. This tag identifies the instrument that is playing the most prominent part. But if we look closely at what is happening in back of the solo, we see 20 strings plus the second guitar playing TREMOLANDO; even if this accompaniment were marked PIANISSIMO, the effect would be that of considerable *weight*. The Spanish guitar speaks quite foltly; consequently, this writing creates an imbalance. Because of the instrumental weight opposing the solo, the soloing guitar will be diminished to the extent that it would be unlikely even to be heard under normal circumstances. Problems such as this are not uncommon, and may be remedied in most cases without modifying the score by judicious placement of a close-pickup microphone. However, the ideal time to consider logistics of this nature is during drafting of the score.

The music sheets of Fig. 6-3 contain many errors of omission. The partial score, written for a smaller group of musicians, denotes a degree of thinness; because of this nakedness, the score should have more complete dynamic markings in order to leave no doubt as to the approach by the individual musicians.

Fig. 6-2. Orchestrated score example at 3½ seconds per bar.

Fig. 6-2. (cont.) Orchestrated score example.

No tempo directive has been given except for the number of seconds allotted to each bar. The first notes are written for muted trombones and stopped horns. This color usually produces the sound of a subdued reaction with a degree of tension, but the horn players will have no idea of whether to play the note loudly, softly, or intermediately. At its best, with no dynamics for the horns and no accent mark for the trombones (granted, they are instructed to play MEZZO FORTE), the attack can be only apologetic.

The vibraphone and harp figure, which is similar to a slow arpeggio, can only be performed as filigree because of the lack of dynamic marking.

Notice next, in the second bar, two clarinets and a bass clarinet making an entrance. These three musicians can only approach these notes cautiously because, again, there is no indication of how the composer wishes the music to be played The piano player doesn't have to second-guess the composer because of the MEZZO PIANO mark in bar 3. The horns and trombones, in the fifth bar, have probably gotten the message by this time in regard to how the music should sound.

Once more, we will probably hear an apologetic entrance of the bass clarinet and contrabass in the seventh bar (not to mention the clarinets and horns).

The eighth bar (sheet B, Fig. 6-3) at least tells the violinists to play softly; but are they to slur the two notes or not?

At last, in the ninth bar (sheet C) something happens to restore the interest of the performers: a CRESCENDO and DECRESCENDO.

We had no indication, in this example, of any important soloistic passages. There are varied colors—muted brass, vibraphone and harp, low woodwinds (dark), low piano, moderately low strings, and an isolated tympani in the twelfth bar.

This type of music should represent no challenge to the reader because of its simplicity and almost innocuous planning. We must assume that it would have more character with the proper application of dynamics and expression marks.

Film recording musicians seem to be uncanny in anticipating and feeling the sense of the music, even with a

Fig. 6-3 (sheet A). Without adequate directorial marks, the score can't really be considered complete. Note absence of tempo directives and general dynamic instruction.

Fig. 6-3 (sheet B). Even if the musicians get the feel of the pacing and dynamics, some are introduced "cold." Should the violins slur the seventh bar?

Fig. 6-3 (sheet C). The crescendo and decrescendo in the ninth bar serve to restore the interest of the performers.

minimum of directive symbols. This also applies to errors in written notes that may appear in the parts. It is not uncommon for musicians to correct errors, at times even before playing the note by listening to the preceding music and anticipating the music to follow. However, a psychological point must be brought out which concerns the interest that the musicians have in performing the music. If the score is ill-prepared, with a minimum of directives, it will always reflect in the performance and make the difference between music that breathes with life and music that is listless, dull, and unimpressive.

Let us examine now three actual scored film vignettes. The purpose of this book is to describe film music from a basic standpoint so that a clear impression can be given as to the function of this music. Every attempt has been made to avoid cliches, unorthodox sounds, and other devices in order to preserve clarity. This is not intended to criticize the use of the many multiple colors in all of the sections of the film orchestra, but rather to simplify analysis of the following examples.

The music accompanying the three selected film segments appears in two forms: a complete orchestral score, and a condensation or transcription of the score into music playable on the piano. Because of the space required to show any appreciable portion of a music score that is fully orchestrated, the music-sheet examples accompanying the vignettes described in this chapter are adapted for the piano. This allows the music to be more readily evaluated by overviewing, and makes it easier to relate the score to the accompanying story line. The orchestrated versions of these passages appear at the end of the chapter. For obvious reasons the piano reductions do not contain all of the elements of the orchestral score.

In certain music scores there appear horizontal lines ending at a given timing (——————————┤). These indicate to the conductor that a white streamer will appear on the screen at that point as an aid to meeting critical timings throughout the sequence.

Furthermore, many blank bars will appear in the scores throughout the sequences. These are *bars rest*. Film composers ignore writing the *rest* symbol in each bar as a timesaver. The copyist will automatically indicate these as bars rest in the extracted orchestral parts.

MATING STORY AND SCORE—EXAMPLE 1

The first example of a wedded story and music score is divided into two parts: the first contains dramatic subtleties, and the second, dramatic action.

This first example deals with the classic female, male, female triangle in a modern western setting. The various dramatic elements include a scenic western opening following which the male third of the triangle tells a homicide detective of dramatic developments that happened previously. In the flashback (the main body of the story line), we find the male (Carl) with Marie (his paramour) in her living room. They are discussing the problems of his acquiring a divorce from his wife (Marian). The action continues with a love scene which is interrupted by a telephone call from Marian. In the one-sided, explosive dialog on the phone, Marian berates Marie and claims that she intends to stampede their large herd of cattle. The after-divorce ownership of the herd is the basis for the dispute between Marian and Carl. After hanging up the phone, Marian grabs a shotgun and speeds off in her convertible to where the cattle are grazing. Meanwhile, Marie and Carl also leave to intercept Marian. Marian arrives at the scene of the grazing herd and fires the gun to create the stampede. After a period she hears the approach of the other automobile, turns around, and fires point-blank at the car. This shatters the windshield, causing the car to skid off the road into a gulley—Marie is thrown from the car and killed. We dissolve back to the homicide office and the segment finishes with Carl's dialog, "...which I guess was some sort of blessing."

The music cue sheet for the initial part of the story is presented in Fig. 6-4. The score itself appears as Fig. 6-5. The score sheet should be examined while referencing the cue sheet. For the following analysis, turn to the appropriate orchestrated score at the end of this chapter.

The music at the beginning of part 1 is fairly stark with a slight sense of movement appearing in the violas and the 2nd clarinet. Attention should be given to the horns; contrary to

MUSIC CUE SHEET

Time	Cue	Description
:00	F.I.	SCENIC WESTERN B.G. DESERT- SNOW CAPPED MOUNTAINS, ETC. DIRT ROAD - NO TRAFFIC
:05⅓		CAR APPEARS IN DISTANCE, TRAVELLING TOWARD CAMERA - MODERATE SPEED
:14⅔		PASSES CAMERA
:16	CUT	C.U. DRIVER OF CAR - WELL DRESSED (TRAVELLING SHOT)
:22	PAN	CAR DISAPPEARING DOWN ROAD
:29⅓	'CUT	MODERN WESTERN CITY STREET - LIGHT TRAFFIC
:33⅓	CUT	SAME CAR TOWARD CAMERA - RUNS BY
:39⅓	CUT	EXT. POLICE DEPARTMENT BUILDING
:43¼		CAR DRIVES UP - STOPS - MAN GETS OUT AND ENTERS BUILDING
:58⅔	CUT	INSERT - OFFICE DOOR MARKED HOMICIDE DIVISION
1:03⅓		MAN ENTERS OFFICE - CAMERA FOLLOWS
1:10	DIAL.	MAN: "HOW ARE YOU ROY?" DETECTIVE: "PRETTY GOOD, CARL, CONSIDERING THE WORK LOAD. (PAUSE) WOULD YOU MIND GIVING ME THE DETAILS?"
1:24		CARL: "WELL, AS YOU KNOW, MARIAN AND I HAD NOT BEEN - SHALL WE SAY, COMPATIBLE FOR TWO OR THREE YEARS. YOU ARE ALSO PROBABLY AWARE OF MY ATTACHMENT TO MARIE. IT ALL STARTED WHILE I WAS OVER AT HER HOUSE, NIGHT BEFORE LAST
1:34		SLOW OIL DISSOLVE OVER FOLLOWING
		"WE WERE TRYING TO COME TO SOME CONCLUSIONS ABOUT HOW TO WORK THINGS OUT........."
1:38		END OF DISSOLVE TO FLASHBACK - MARIE'S LIVING ROOM (WELL APPOINTED). MARIE AND CARL SITTING CLOSE ON SOFA - HIS ARM AROUND HER
1:40⅔	DIAL.	MARIE: "HAVE YOU TALKED TO HER AGAIN ABOUT A DIVORCE? CARL: "JUST THIS MORNING, AND STILL THE SAME ANSWER...ONLY IF I GIVE HER THE CATTLE. I CAN'T DO THAT BECAUSE, AS YOU KNOW, I STARTED THE WHOLE SPREAD LONG BEFORE I KNEW HER AND I SEE NO REASON WHY I SHOULDN'T RETAIN....
1:56		SHE INTERRUPTS, PUTTING HIS FACE BETWEEN HER HANDS
1:56⅔	DIAL.	MARIE: "NOW, NOW DARLING. WE WILL FIND SOME WAY" - SHE KISSES HIM PASSIONATELY
2:03⅓	DIAL.	MARIE: "AFTER ALL I DO LOVE YOU DEARLY. CARL: "AND I YOU."
2:08⅔		THEY CONTINUE TORRID EMBRACE
2:14	SOUND	TELEPHONE RINGING - 3 TIMES
2:20	DIAL.	MARIE: " DAMN!" SHE GOES TO PHONE
2:24⅔	DIAL.	MARIE: "HELLO"

Fig. 6-4. Music cue sheet for the first part of story, example 1.

amplifying the violas and clarinet, they will act as a legato cover so that the movement will not be too pronounced. The same thing applies to the vibraphone trill.

The first clarinet enters in bar 3 playing a solo in the high register. This is to convey a feeling of lonesome openness in the desert scene. It should be noted that no attempt is made to point up the scenic snowcapped mountain background, it being assumed that the photography will be of sufficient impact to preclude the need for music assistance (or competition).

The traveling car and shot of the driver is ignored musically to avoid tipping off the audience to a dramatic development that has not as yet been disclosed.

In bar 13 the background movement (violas and English horn) accompanying the two flutes is a bit more intense, but not enough to signal any important dramatic change; rather, it is a logical development in the music construction.

A change in dramatic values finally appears in the 17th bar. This is intended to convey a smooth transition to the police department building. It should be observed that no musical impact is given on the cut to the building. Immediately following the cut in the 19th bar we find a respectful, almost sombre feeling in the music. This music increases in weight with some intensity up to the point of dialog within the 29th bar. Here we notice a drop in weight and movement in order to protect the dialog. Nevertheless, the tension does increase once again with Carl's dialog disclosing the dramatic developments that follow.

Although the 37th and 38th bars may be considered musical "footwork" (backing the slow dissolve to the flashback), it is an expected device that could be written in dozens of different ways. The sole purpose is to afford a musical transition erasing the former music function and preparing for the scene to follow.

The romantic period, starting at the 39th bar, has music constructed from a fragmentary motif which describes the warmth between the two characters. If the music had been written describing the obvious tension at the beginning of the scene, the ultimate passionate embrace, with appropriate music, would certainly run the risk of being highly melodramatic or even corny.

Fig. 6-5 (sheet A). Piano adaptation of score used in story (part 1) of example 1. (Orchestrated version at end of chapter.)

Fig. 6-5 (sheet B).

137

Fig. 6-5 (sheet C).

Fig. 6-5 (sheet D).

In bar 53 the change to a dark orchestral color describes the interruption and disappointment caused by the telephone ringing. The held note (FERMATA) in the final bar will be taken over by the incoming music of part 2.

In reviewing the first half of this scene we find no excessive music punctuations, notwithstanding the *dissolve* music. Instead, it contains subtle changes in colors and values and attempts to avoid dramatic impact where actually none was present.

Figure 6-6 is the music cue sheet for the second part of our initial example. The tension of this scene obviously requires a different music approach than that used earlier. Figure 6-7, the piano-adapted version of the score, shows how the music relates to the filmed action with respect to elapsed time. For the orchestral analysis, however, refer to the appropriate music sheets at the end of this chapter.

At the beginning of the second part of example 1, we find low ominous dark colors with very little movement in contrast to the violent, hysterical dialog. In bar 6, notice that the action-type music precedes the slam of the phone receiver. This is intentional in order to avoid a *direct music cue* with the sound of the receiver. It also conveys an impetus for her action. From this point on, the heavy dramatic music, with its faster tempo, parallels the wife's hysteria and its effect on Marie and Carl. This continues until bar 30 (the cut to the

```
                          MUSIC CUE SHEET

 :00    DIAL.    MARIE: "HELLO"

        DIAL.    FEMALE VOICE AT OTHER END OF LINE
                 "WELL, YOU BITCH - TELL THAT BASTARD
                 HUSBAND OF MINE, WHO'S PROBABLY IN BED
                 WITH YOU, THAT HE DOESN'T HAVE TO WORRY
                 ABOUT HIS DAMN CATTLE ANY MORE. WHEN I
                 HANG UP THIS PHONE I'M ON MY WAY OUT TO
                 THE HERD AND I INTEND TO STAMPEDE ALL OF
                 THEM. LET HIM GO OUT AND TRY TO ROUND
                 THEM UP!"

 :16⅔   CUT      WIFE SLAMMING DOWN RECEIVER. SHE RUSHES
                 OVER TO GUN RACK - GRABS A SHOTGUN AND
                 RUNS OUT OF HOUSE TO CONVERTIBLE - JUMPS
                 IN AND ROARS OFF

 :36    CUT      MARIE AND CARL. DIAL. CARL: "SHE CAN'T
                 DO IT. I MUST STOP HER!"

 :39⅓            HE RUSHES TO DOOR - MARIE AFTER HIM

 :43⅓   DIAL.    CARL: "NO - YOU STAY HERE
                 MARIE: "I CERTAINLY WILL NOT."
                 CARL: "THIS COULD BE LOTS OF TROUBLE AND
                 I CAN'T....
                 MARIE: DON'T JUST STAND THERE ARGUING.
                 GET IN THE CAR."

 :51⅓            THEY RUN TO CAR - GET IN AND MAKE A WHEEL
                 SPINNING EXIT DOWN THE ROAD.

 1:03⅓  CUT      LARGE HERD OF CATTLE GRAZING

 1:08⅔  SOUND    O.S. GUNSHOTS - HERD BEGINS TO RUN

 1:18   CUT      CAR DOWN ROAD AT SPEED. WIFE FIRING GUN
                 IN AIR

 1:23⅓  CUT      MARIE AND CARL IN OTHER CAR - SPEEDING
                 ALONG ROAD

 1:28⅔           VARIOUS CUTS OF HERD AT FULL STAMPEDE

 1:41⅓  CUT      WIFE'S CAR APPROACHING REAR OF STAMPEDING
                 CATTLE — STILL FIRING

 1:48            BRINGS CAR TO STOP

 1:51⅓  SOUND    WIFE HEARS CAR APPROACHING IN DISTANCE
                 SHE STANDS UP AND LOOKS BACK

 1:54⅔  CUT      OTHER CAR - WIFE'S POV

 1:57⅓  CUT      WIFE LAUGHING HYSTERICALLY - POINTS GUN
                 AND FIRES DIRECTLY AT OTHER CAR

 2:00   CUT      WINDSHIELD SHATTERING

 2:02   CUT      MAN'S FOOT HITTING BRAKE PEDAL
        SOUND    SCREAMING TIRES

 2:03⅔  CUT      CAR SKIDDING OFF ROAD INTO SHALLOW GULLY

 2:06⅔           MARIE THROWN OUT - LAND ON ROCKS ON SIDE
                 OF GULLY

 2:11⅓           SLOW OIL DISSOLVE BACK TO OFFICE

 2:14   DIAL.    CARL: "WELL, ROY, YOU KNOW THE REST.
                 MARIE MUST HAVE DIED INSTANTLY, WHICH,
                 I GUESS WAS SOME SORT OF BLESSING

                                      ABBREVIATIONS
                                      O.S.—OFF STAGE
                                      POV—POINT OF VIEW
```

Fig. 6-6. Music cue sheet for second part of story example 1.

Fig. 6-7 sheet A). Piano adaptation of score used in story, part 2 of example 1. (Orchestrated version at end of chapter.)

Fig. 6-7 (sheet B).

Fig. 6-7 (sheet C).

Fig. 6-7 (sheet D).

cattle) where a placid change describes the scene. Following the gunshots in bar 32 the music once again punctuates the dramatic impact that is indicated in the scenes and cuts. Notice that the music does not employ a strict rhythmic structure and so does not interfere with the sounds of the stampeding cattle. The music agitation ceases when the car stops in bar 48. This is planned for two reasons: to describe the tension going on within the wife, and to allow the offstage sound of the approaching car to be heard without music interference. Pandemonium sets in from bar 53 through bar 58 as amplification of the heavy, tragic drama that unfolds. Bars 59 and 60 finish the sequence with a transition to dialog in the police station.

MATING STORY AND SCORE—EXAMPLE 2

Example 2 is less involved; it depicts a burglary at night in which the thief is apprehended by a little blind girl. The child, descending a darkened staircase, senses the presence of the thief. After calling frantically for her father, who rushes down the stairs with drawn gun, the thief, in attempting to escape, stumbles over a light cord and is restrained by the father. The example finishes with the father directing the child to call the police. The final scene is a closeup of her fingers seeking out the proper dial holes on the instrument.

The music cue sheet for this vignette appears as Fig. 6-8. The piano adaptation of the score is Fig. 6-9. The full score, referenced in the following analysis, appears at the end of the chapter.

This example is a sequence with very sparse dialog—only three lines by the child and three by the father. Along with this, there is a minimum of sound effects. In other words, the music is depended upon to carry the atmosphere *and tempo* of the entire scene. The piano chord, at the beginning, is intended to convey a chilled feeling in describing the scene. Added to this is the Yamaha portamento ribbon controller which slowly glides back and forth in a narrow interval span. Each new color is added unobtrusively (vibraphone and strings, without vibrato) in order to give the feeling of slowly moving fog.

The first conscious feeling of movement is played by the cello section in bar 7. Nonetheless, they will be performing *pianissimo* with mutes which should sound more like a low whisper. The approach of the car in bar 13 is ignored by the music, with a slight punctuation appearing in bar 15 to denote the relief of the man at not being seen. In the 17th bar, the color darkens considerably and gives a foreboding, mysterious quality. This continues to bar 37 in which, following the cut upstairs, the clarinet solo describes the hesitancy of the child walking along the corridor. This music function builds as she walks slowly down the stairs. It continues to the 44th bar, where we notice a direct cutoff in the music. This should have an even more forceful effect than a heavy accent on the cut to the robber. At this point it should be explained that the dynamic markings in bar 44 (L.P. and LUNGA) are the same directive; L.P. means *long pause*, and is used generally in film music, whereas *lunga* is the more formal phrase.

:00	F.I.	FOGGY NIGHT (LIKE LONDON) - NARROW WET STREET - DIM STREET LIGHTS - WEIRD SHADOWS, ETC.
:08		MAN MOVES SLOWLY OUT OF DARK - WE DO NOT SEE HIS FACE
:15⅔		CAMERA FOLLOWS HIM AROUND CORNER AND DOWN ANOTHER, WIDER STREET
:27		HE ARRIVES AT SMALL PARK AT THE FAR SIDE OF WHICH IS LARGE HOME.
:30⅔	SOUND	DISTANT CAR APPROACHING - MAN DUCKS INTO DOORWAY UNTIL CAR PASSES
:37⅓		HE CROSSES PARK AND GOES TO GATE OF HOUSE
:52⅔		SILENTLY OPENS GATE AND ENTERS
:56	DIS.	DARKENED LIBRARY IN HOUSE - CAMERA PANS OVER TO WINDOW
1:00		WINDOW OPENS, MAN CLIMBS IN - FLASHLIGHT SCANS WALL
1:10		STOPS ON PICTURE - MAN MOVES UP, PULLS HINGED PICTURE FROM WALL EXPOSING
1:19⅓		SAFE
1:22	CUT	HANDS WORKING DIAL FOR COMBINATION
1:33⅔		OPENS SAFE - ROBBER WITHDRAWS CONTENTS
1:37⅓	CUT	UPSTAIRS. SMALL 6 OR 7 YEAR OLD CHILD WALKING SLOWLY ALONG CORRIDOR TO STAIRS (IT HAS BEEN ESTABLISHED THAT SHE IS BLIND)
1:46		SHE WALKS SLOWLY DOWN STAIRS (HAND ON RAIL)
1:54⅔	CUT	ROBBER
1:56		HE SEES HER - TURNS OFF FLASHLIGHT
1:59⅓	CUT	CHILD
2:01⅓		CHILD STOPS HALFWAY DOWN STAIRS
2:02	DIAL.	"IS SOMEONE THERE?" PAUSE "I FEEL THAT SOMEONE IS DOWN THERE!" SCREAMS "FATHER!"
2:09⅓	CUT	BEDROOM - FATHER OUT OF BED - GRABS ROBE
2:16	CUT	LIBRARY - ROBBER MOVING SLOWLY TOWARD WINDOW
2:18	DIAL O.S.	CHILD: "WHO IS IT - WHO IS IT?"
2:22⅔	CUT	FATHER RUNNING DOWN STEPS - PISTOL IN HAND
2:28	CUT	ROBBER TRIPS OVER LIGHT CORD
2:30⅔	CUT	FATHER SWITCHES ON LIGHTS AT FOOT OF STAIRS - POINTS PISTOL
2:31⅓	DIAL.	"HOLD IT, HOLD IT RIGHT THERE - PUT YOUR HANDS OVER YOUR HEAD!" WALKS SLOWLY OVER TO ROBBER
2:34⅔	DIAL.	FATHER TO CHILD - "DIAL THE POLICE - THE NUMBER IS 345-7991"
2:40⅔	C.U.	CHILD'S FINGER FEELING FOR NUMBERS AND DIALING.
2:51⅓		END SCENE

Fig. 6-8. Music cue sheet for example 2.

This long pause allows the child's screams to have even more impact than if they were accompanied by music. The quickening tempo and fast movement starting in bar 45

Fig. 6-9 (sheet A). Piano adaptation of score used in story example 2.

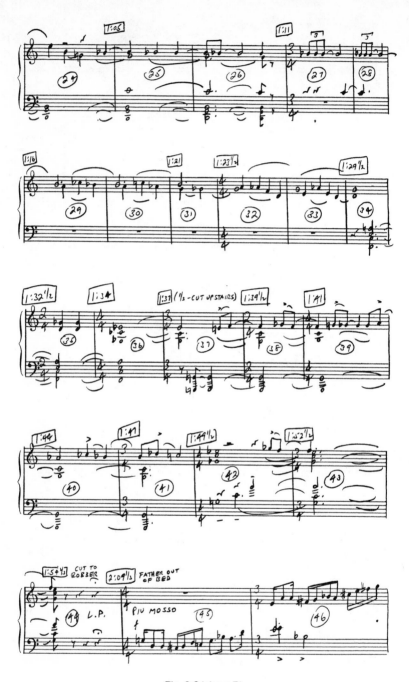

Fig. 6-9 (sheet B).

Fig. 6-9 (sheet C).

denote the father's anxiety while rushing to the aid of his daughter. The first heavy punctuation appears in the 54th bar when the robber trips over the light cord. The music then tapers off to the end of the sequence.

MATING STORY AND SCORE—EXAMPLE 3

The final vignette, example 3, is taken from an actual happening some years ago in a big city. It involved the mugging-murder of a young woman in full view of many apartment dwellers, not one of whom offered assistance. When questioned by the police, onlookers gave no information as to the identity of the assailant, even though he had been recognized by at least one couple who had watched the tragic event from a nearby tenement window.

The music cue sheet of Fig. 6-10 depicts the timing and sequence of events. An overview of the music is provided in the piano adaptation of Fig. 6-11. The orchestrated score appears at the end of the chapter.

The establishing music in this scene is a distant hurdy-gurdy, or grind organ, with the functional music entering at 10 seconds, playing in juxtaposition to the street organ throughout the entire sequence. As the hurdy-gurdy music will be on a separate track, and not recorded at the same time with the scoring orchestra, the functional music timings begin with :00. The music editor will apply the two tracks in the proper sequence at a later time.

The hurdy-gurdy playing against the orchestra is, of course, not a new device. In fact, the establishing music could be either a radio or muted piano sound coming from one of the apartments. However, the monotonous sound of the grind organ tends to allow more latitude in the music that is superimposed.

The street organ music is not intended as realistic or source music because it is rare that one hears such instruments anymore. Rather, it is intended as a reminiscent sound associated with the area. It also creates conflict in the scene of the uncooperative witnesses following the murder.

In analyzing the orchestral music we find no appreciable characteristics in the writing in the first 11 bars. The crescendo in bar 12 simply acts as a transition of the man

150

```
                        MUSIC CUE SHEET

START HURDY-GURDY.  NEW YORK TENEMENT DISTRICT - EARLY EVENING -
                    HOT - MEN AND WOMEN AT OPEN WINDOWS, GOSSIPING
                    WITH NEIGHBORS - VARIOUS SHOTS - NO TRAFFIC.

    :00    (:10)    OVERLAY ORCHESTRA

    :08    CUT      YOUNG WOMAN HURRIEDLY WALKING DOWN STREET.
                    CLUTCHING PURSE UNDER HER ARM.

    :17⅓            PASSES GROUP. OF MALE YOUTHS ON STEPS. THEY
                    MAKE INSULTING REMARKS - "HEY CHICK, WATCHA DOIN',
                    DRUMMIN' UP BUSINESS"? - ETC.
                    SHE CONTINUES - CAMERA PRECEDING HER.

    :30⅔            PASSES ONE TENEMENT - NO ONE ON STEPS.

    :32             MAN RUNS OUT FROM SHADOWS.

    :34             TRIES TO GRAB PURSE - THEY STRUGGLE, SHE
                    SCREAMS

    :38⅔   CUT      WINDOWS - TENENTS WATCHING SILENTLY - WOMAN'S
                    SCREAMS OVER

    :43⅓   CUT      BACK TO STRUGGLE

    :45⅓            MAN HITS HER ON HEAD WITH BLACKJACK - SHE
                    COLLAPSES

    :48             QUICK CUTS TO TENENTS, FROZEN

    :52    CUT      MAN HITTING HER AGAIN AND AGAIN - HE GRABS
                    PURSE AND RUNS

    :58⅔            HOLD ON GIRL ON SIDEWALK IN POOL OF BLOOD

   1:03⅓  CUT      TWO TENENTS STARING - WOMAN WHISPERS

   1:04⅔           "DO YOU KNOW WHO HE WAS?"

   1:07⅓           HUSBAND: "YEAH, JOHNNY FELICIO FROM DOWN THE
                    BLOCK."

                    WIFE: "SHOULDN'T WE CALL THE POLICE?"

                    HUSBAND: "NO - WE'LL KEEP OUT OF THIS AND YOU
                    KEEP YOUR TRAP SHUT."

   1:17⅓           END DIALOGUE - HUSBAND PULLS DOWN SHADE AND
                    TURNS OFF LIGHT

                    CUTS TO OTHER TENENTS DOING SAME

   1:31⅓  CUT      PATROL CAR CRUISING SLOWLY DOWN STREET

   1:36⅔           STOPS BY WOMAN - OFFICERS RUSH OVER TO WOMAN
                    AND EXAMINE HER

   1:52   DIAL.    1ST OFFICER: "SHE'S DEAD"
                    2ND OFFICER TO CAR TO CALL AMBULANCE
                    1ST OFFICER UP STEPS OF TENEMENT

   2:03⅓  CUT      INSIDE HALL - OFFICER ENTERS AND KNOCKS ON
                    DOOR—NO RESPONSE - CONTINUES KNOCKING, CALLS
                    "THIS IS THE POLICE" MAN OPENS DOOR. OFFICER
                    QUESTIONS MAN ABOUT WITNESSING EVENT. MAN
                    ANSWERS "I DIDN'T HEAR OR SEE A THING."

   2:26            SHORT MONTAGE - OFFICER AT OTHER DOORS - ALL
                    NEGATIVE ANSWERS - OFFICER FINALLY LEAVES AND
                    RETURNS TO CAR.

   2:50   DIAL.    2ND OFFICER: "GET ANY INFORMATION?"
                    1ST OFFICER: "NO - THE SAME STORY NOBODY
                    KNOWS NOTHING."

   2:57⅓           FADE OUT ORCHESTRA UNDER SOUND OF AMBULANCE
                    CONTINUE HURDY-GURDY TO END OF SEQUENCE
```

Fig. 6-10. Music cue sheet for story example 3.

Fig. 6-11 (sheet A). Piano adaptation of score used in story example 3.

running out and frightening the girl. Without this, the shock effect in bar 13 could border on the melodramatic. This is a valid approach because we can assume that the only sound effects would be the man's running footsteps, the girl's screams, and the hit on the head with the blackjack. During this period the hurdy-gurdy could be blocked out by the hysteria in the orchestral music.

Fig. 6-11 (sheet B).

Bars 26 through 31 denote an almost mysterious, questioning feeling to accompany the dialog. With the shades being lowered (bar 32 through the first half of bar 35) we find stark drama with an almost sympathetic quality.

The use of the clarinet and oboe solos, bars 37 through 39, should give a feeling of questioning or curiosity while the officer goes to the body to investigate. The bass clarinet solo,

Fig. 6-11 (sheet C).

with its dark color in bars 40 and 41, should be noted. Also, no music punctuation is indicated in the 42nd bar under the officer's line, "She's dead."

Movement begins in bar 43 to accompany the officer up the steps and through the hall in anticipation of possible witnesses. The fruitless search is described with the falling off of the weight in the orchestra and lapsing into a feeling of

154

Fig. 6-11 (sheet D).

disappointment and shock in the refusal of the apartment dwellers to cooperate.

As indicated, the street organ continues, after the orchestra ceases, until the end of the sequence, thus giving a feeling of life going on as usual.

Example 1, part 1 (from Figs. 6-4 and 6-5).

163

167

169

171

172

174

176

177

178

179

180

181

182

Example 2 (from Figs. 6-8 and 6-9).

186

187

189

192

193

195

196

197

199

Example 3 (from Figs. 6-10 and 6-11).

203

205

207

208

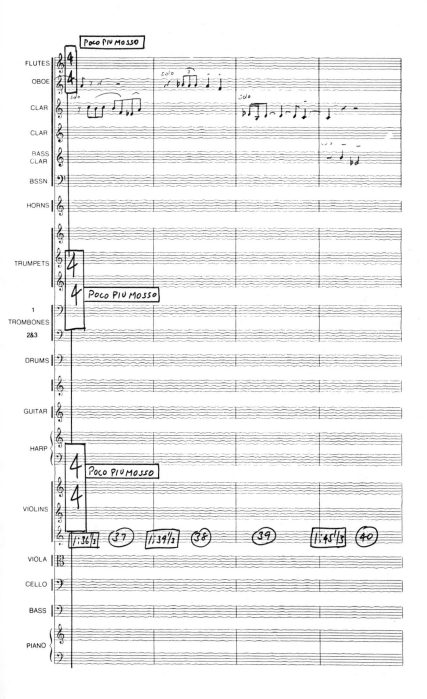

209

210

211

214

215

Appendixes

Postproduction Logistics

The *Copyright* material included in the following text is excerpted from a lecture given by Abraham Marcus in the Telecommunication and Film department at San Diego State University. Mr. Marcus is a member of the law firm of Zissu, Marcus, Stein, and Couture, counselors for *Screen Composers Association of America* as well as the *Composers and Lyricists Guild of America*. Mr. Marcus' familiarization with the many seemingly complicated functions following music postrecording for film indicates that no better source of information is available.

NONSTATUTORY COPYRIGHT

The creator of an intellectual property—a book, lecture, music, etc.—has the right to its exclusive ownership; no one can use it without his consent. But once he publishes it, it falls into the public domain (anyone can copy or use it) unless it is protected by statutory copyright. Although the performance of a play which had not been printed or published has been held not to constitute an abandonment to public use, the courts have held that the manufacture, sale, and distribution to the public of phonograph records does constitute *publication*, which will forfeit the common-law proprietary rights to the music on copyright. Some well regarded legal writers have suggested that any public exploitation of an intellectual work will put it into the public domain unless it is protected by statutory copyright, which involves certain formalities, including affixing the © notice or actual registration in the U.S. copyright office.

STATUTORY COPYRIGHT

Throughout most of the world there are laws for the protection of intellectual property—which in effect provide a monopoly in the work for the creator or his assignee—for all uses of the work.

In this country the basis for statutory protection is found in the United States Constitution, Article 1, Section 8, Clause 8, which grants to the U.S. congress the power "to promote the progress of science and useful arts by securing for limited times to authors and inventors the exclusive right to their respective writings and discoveries."

The present U.S. copyright law was enacted in 1909 (replacing predecessor laws going back to the prior century) and has been amended from time to time since then. Repeated efforts over the last 15 years or so of all the interests affected by copyright to obtain a new revised overall copyright law have foundered on the conflict between copyright proprietors and creators on one side and the various users on the other.

The 1909 act gives to the creator or his assignee certain exclusive rights for a period of 28 years with a renewal period of an additional 28 years.

Among the protected works are motion picture photoplays [Sec. 5 (1)], motion pictures other than photoplays [Sec. 5 (m)], dramatico-musical compositions [Sec. 5 (d)], musical compositions [Sec. 5 (e)], and composite works [Sec. 3]. Although the last mentioned section provides, and the intent of the act seems clearly to be, that all component parts of the copyrighted work are protected by the copyright of the composite work, there recently has been some doubt expressed as to whether the soundtrack of a motion picture is protected by the copyright of the motion picture. As to music, it is simple to copyright that separately—and it should be done, since it costs but a small registration fee plus a copy of the music.

The statutory copyright goes to the author or proprietor or his assignees (Sec. 9), and an employer for hire is included in the definition of "author" (Sec. 26), the latter being of importance in motion picture production. It is to be noted that the copyright in the intellectual work exists separately from the physical object. The copyright law provides in Section 28 that:

> The copyright is distinct from the property in the material object copyrighted, and the sale or conveyance...of the material object shall not of itself constitute a transfer of the copyright, nor shall the assignment of the copyright constitute a transfer of title to the material object...

Therefore, the purchase of a sheet of music does not give you the right to perform it or to copy it or to manufacture a phonograph record from it. Likewise, the purchase of a motion picture does not carry with it the right to exhibit it, unless it is specially granted otherwise.

FILM MUSIC AS A SOURCE OF REVENUE

After there have been combined in a motion picture the elements of idea, script, actors, photography, and all the other elements which result in a motion picture, there is a product which can be sold or leased for exhibition or television broadcast. It is an integrated work which can be marketed in various ways.

There is, however, an important element of the picture which can be a source of revenue independent from the exhibition or broadcast of the motion picture itself: the public performance for profit of the music, which is performed by the soundtrack when the picture is exhibited or broadcast.

THE PERFORMING RIGHTS SOCIETIES

The right to public performance of a work appears to have been recognized in France as early as 1791. In 1851 there was formed, in France, an organization known as *Societe d'Auteurs, Compositeurs et Editors de Musique* (SACEM) for the purpose of licensing, for a fee, the right to perform the music of its composer, author, and publisher members.

The idea of having an organization which would collect from the users of music a fee for the right to perform it spread to England in the early part of this century, and to this country in about 1914. In that year Victor Herbert, other successful songwriters, and the leading music publishers of the day combined in an organization known as *The American Society of Composers, Authors and Publishers*, now commonly referred to as ASCAP, in order to collect fees for the public performance, for profit, of their works.

Throughout the world today (at least so far as our Western and European civilizations are concerned) there exist organizations whose purpose is to license and collect fees for the public performance of the copyrighted works. There are cross-licensing arrangements between the various national societies so that when a work is performed in a country foreign to its author and publisher, the performing rights organization of that country will collect for that performance and transmit the fee to the organization in the other country with which the author and publisher are affiliated.

So far as American works are concerned, both the domestic and the foreign collection is only for public performance of the music. In a number of foreign countries the collection is for both the music and the story. This is the result of the history of the performing rights, where the producer of American films grants the performing rights when licensing the picture. The right to perform the music is not granted, because of the existence of the American societies for the collection of the performing fees for the music.

In the foreign countries there exists only one society in each country for the collection and licensing of performance rights of music. This is because the foreign societies are recognized and supported by the country and its laws. In this country ASCAP was the original music performing rights society and it established, by a series of lawsuits, its right to collect fees for the public performance for profit of the music in its repertory.

The form of ASCAP's organization is that of an unincorporated voluntary association of composers, authors, and publishers, and originally it took exclusive assignments for a period of years as a condition of membership.

Its collections began about ten years after its formation (i.e., about 1924) and it currently collects about $70 million per year. Its method of distribution is to deduct administrative expense and then divide the balance equally between its publisher members on the one hand, and the writers (i.e., authors and composers) on the other.

Not too long after ASCAP's successful establishment of a system of collecting performance fees for the public performance for profit of the music of its members, the broadcasters (at that time, radio only) complained to the Department of Justice that the ASCAP organization and method of operations violated the antitrust laws. It was true that at the time the only organization for the collection of performance fees for music was ASCAP. It was also true that all the music publishers and all the composers were members. There was no other way, as a practical matter, that composers or publishers could collect for the performance of their works other than by a nationwide organization, which had to encompass all or practically all of the music in the country.

An antitrust suit was instituted by the United States against ASCAP as early as 1935.

In addition to stimulating the government to bring its antitrust suit, the radio networks formed their own performing rights organization known as *Broadcast Music, Inc.* (BMI). Its purpose was to create an effective competitor to ASCAP. It is a corporation of which the sole stockholders are those interests having broadcast licenses. Although originally the large chain broadcasters were the primary stockholders, they have disposed of their stock interest so that the stock is now owned by various small broadcasting organizations. Although organized as a profitmaking organization, its articles of incorporation provide that no dividends will ever be paid.

The government's antitrust suit against ASCAP resulted in a consent decree in 1941 which was amended in 1950 and again in 1960. The antitrust decree as amended has resulted in ASCAP being now controlled by the government in every aspect of its operations, even to a greater extent than public utilities. Under the antitrust decree, ASCAP may not deny membership to a composer or publisher who meets the very minimum requirements for membership. The rates which it may charge to users for the use of the music of its members is controlled by the district court in New York which has jurisdiction of any difference between the user and ASCAP as to the amount of rates to be charged. Distributions by ASCAP to its members are likewise controlled by rules determined in the most recent antitrust decree. In this connection, monitors appointed by the court supervise the method of making distributions and the Department of Justice must be consulted at each step in connection with the changes.

Most important from the point of view of the motion picture producer was the private lawsuit by a chain of exhibitors which was begun in 1942 and finally ended in about 1949. In this case, the exhibitors sought an injunction against ASCAP's collection of fees for the performance of music in the motion pictures in their theatres. The claim was made that the ASCAP organization was a violation of the antitrust laws in that it was a combination of composers, authors, publishers, and motion picture producers who owned several of the largest music publishing companies. When the case went to trial, the court agreed that ASCAP was indeed in violation of the antitrust laws, and after a considerable amount of maneuvering, a decree was entered prohibiting ASCAP or its members from collecting fees for the public performance for profit of the music in motion pictures exhibited in theatres. This injunction, of course, applied only in the private lawsuit, but it was extended, generally, by the 1950 amendment of the consent decree so that since that time ASCAP has made no collections from the motion picture theatres, except for either the live or recorded performance of music other than on the soundtrack of the motion picture.

Although the music in the motion picture does not produce any income via ASCAP for performance in theatres in this country, there is no such limitation on collections in foreign countries. Collections by ASCAP's affiliated societies in foreign countries continue for the music in motion pictures exhibited in those countries. The lack of collections from theatres in this country is a source of annoyance to foreign composers and publishers because the collections abroad are substantial.

ASCAP continues to collect for the performance of motion pictures broadcast by television. Although there have been attempts from time to time by broadcasting interests to oppose the collection of fees for the performance of the music in motion pictures broadcast on television, this opposition has thus far been directed obliquely (and unsuccessfully) by requests for rates to be fixed by the district court for music excluding the music recorded on the soundtrack of motion pictures or television motion pictures. There have been other attacks on ASCAP and BMI based upon the antitrust laws, but these seem to be maneuvering devices in order to obtain satisfactory negotiated rate agreements.

A recent decision at a U.S. court of appeals has held that the terms of the consent decree have so "disinfected" ASCAP that it can no longer be successfully sued in a private civil suit by a user for violation of the antitrust laws.

ASCAP licenses the performance of the music in the motion pictures broadcast by television, and pays to the composers, authors, and publishers of such music distributions from its receipts based upon the performance of such music. BMI also has a repertoire of motion picture music which it began to acquire in competition with ASCAP in about 1960. It, likewise, licenses the performance of the music in motion pictures exhibited on television, collects for it, and distributes to the composers, authors, and publishers affiliated with it.

THE PRODUCER'S PERFORMING RIGHTS INCOME

ASCAP, BMI, and their affiliated foreign societies make payments to only those composers and publishers who are either members of or affiliated with the society or one of its affiliates.

In the case of ASCAP, since it is an association, we refer to the composers, authors, and publishers as members. Since BMI is a corporation, and the relationship with the composers, authors, and publishers is by contract only, they are referred to either as publisher affiliates or writer affiliates.

Insofar as background music is concerned (and when we talk about motion picture music, we are primarily referring to background music in the motion picture), both BMI and ASCAP pay half to the writers and half to the publishers, whether the income is from foreign or domestic sources. The writers can only collect from the American societies for the foreign receipts because of the performance of their music. The foreign societies transmit the money to ASCAP or BMI, depending upon the membership affiliation of the composer; the American society in turn distributes to the writer.

The publisher member or affiliate has its choice either to collect from the American societies or to authorize a foreign publisher to collect in the country generating the performing rights income. Most publishing companies will have a foreign subpublisher collect the performance income and transmit it, less a collection fee, to the American publisher. The reason for this is twofold. First, it is generally thought that a resident publisher in the foreign country will earn his commission (generally about 15%) in supervising the accounts of the local performing rights society and making sure that the particular motion picture is properly paid for; and, secondly, if there is music which can be exploited apart from the motion picture, the local publisher should have some incentive to exploit.

For the American producer to participate in or receive the publisher's share of the distributions from ASCAP and BMI, he must either have a music publishing company which is a member of ASCAP or affiliated with BMI, or he can make a contractual arrangement with a publisher who is a member or affiliate for the collection of the publisher's share of the performance monies. Every major motion picture distributor has two music publishing subsidiaries, one a member of ASCAP and the other affiliated with BMI. The necessity for two publishing houses arises from the fact that in order to have a free choice of composers without being concerned about their performing rights affiliation, it is necessary to have two companies. The networks likewise have their publishing subsidiaries or affiliates.

SOUNDTRACK RECORDINGS

Motion picture soundtrack albums have a twofold importance to the motion picture producer. In the first place, a successful album of motion picture music is a good exploitation tool for the distribution of phonograph records and itself can be a source of a great deal of revenue.

The producer, under the usual contracts through which he obtains the music for the motion picture, has the right to cause the manufacture and sale of soundtrack record albums. If the producer has an affiliated or subsidiary record manufacturing company, it effectively realizes the profit from the sale of the album. Under existing industry customs, when the phonograph record is sold the royalty payable to the publisher of the music is divided with the composer. In addition, composers who are in great demand will be able to obtain from the producer of the motion picture an *artist's royalty*, a percentage of the retail list price of all records sold, manufactured, and paid for. The soundtrack album from *The Sound of Music*, in which Julie Andrews had a record artist's royalty, sold 7 million copies at an average retail price of over $5 which means a sale of $35 million upon which her royalty was based. That figure is hearsay, but it does seem appropriate and logical in view of the fact that the music and the artist were very popular, and the picture was a musical with many songs.

The soundtrack album is worth getting as a matter of exploitation alone, and if it should become successful on its own, it can produce very substantial revenue.

DERIVATION WORKS

In addition to the soundtrack record album, there are other forms in which the music can be exploited with profit to the producer and to his subsidiary or affiliated music publisher. This would be in the area of songs or various arrangements of music taken from the motion picture score. There is a vast area in which sheet music can be exploited. Although sales of piano and vocal copies is relatively small, there is a tremendous market in educational forms of printing, such as arrangements for band, vocal, concert, and symphonic performances.

When these derivative works are exploited by obtaining phonograph records and by obtaining performances, they yield additional income, and these sources can be substantial. A hit song not only can produce large amounts of money immediately, but if the song becomes a standard and continues to be popular, it can continue to bring in record royalty and performance payments.

COMPOSERS' ORGANIZATIONS

We have heretofore discussed the performing rights societies, ASCAP and BMI. Apart from the technical differences in organizational character, the producer should be aware of some of the effects of this difference. ASCAP's basic principle is dividing all of its money after expenses into two equal shares, one to the publisher and one to the composer. There is no way of negotiating with ASCAP for any specific amount to be paid to a member; the member receives the amount determined by the rules of the organization. It is possible, however, for a publisher (as well as a writer) to obtain some advances from ASCAP. These are computed upon the basis of the expected income from specific music scores known to be controlled by the publisher.

BMI, having a different type of organization, makes contractual deals with its affiliates and, in many cases, will offer producers of motion pictures either a guarantee against the amounts to be earned by the music in the motion pictures, or advances to be charged against future earnings. A producer may very often find that the guarantee will do a good deal to pay his music costs during production. Another organization of which the producer should be aware, although he will have no contact with it, is the *Screen Composers Association of the United States of America.* This is an organization of composers of backgound music, formed about 1945 to obtain larger distributions from ASCAP for the performance of background music. Computation of the amounts received for background music, whether publisher or composer, today indicates it is 30 times what would have been if the formula applicable in 1945 had continued to be applied to performances of background music. The publisher and producer of motion pictures have thus been the beneficiary of the activities of the background music composers to increase the amount paid for the performance of their music in motion pictures.

The Composers
Speak Out

During the course of this book's preparation, I interviewed some of the most influential individuals in music today. Much of what they had to say has been incorporated into the body of this book. This appendix is a compilation of additional remarks, ideas, reflections, and opinions of Quincy Jones, Hugo Friedhofer, David Grusin, John Green, Alex North, and Arthur Morton.

In the text that follows, boldface type is used for my questions; composer responses appear in lightface Roman type.

QUINCY JONES

Quincy Jones, one of Hollywood's most successful and sought-after composers, is a product of the jazz school. Close friend and early associate of Ray Charles and other jazz greats, Quincy Jones studied classical composition with Nadia Boulanger in Paris. Upon his return to the United States he began a seven-year association with **Mercury Records**, during which time he became vice-president. During this period, his album arranging credits included many great singers such as

Sammy Davis, Jr., Sarah Vaughan; Frank Sinatra, and Andy Williams.

His Hollywood film career began with his score for *The Pawnbroker* and encompassed 32 film scores in a nine-year period, including *Heat of the Night; In Cold Blood; For the Love of Ivy; Bob, Carol, Ted and Alice; Cactus Flower;* and *The Anderson Tapes.*

Mr. Jones' TV credits include *The Bill Cosby Show, Ironside,* and *Sanford and Son,* among many others.

He is most articulate and I am deeply grateful for the following interview recorded at his Beverly Hills home on February 23, 1972.

Would you care to give your impression of the general status of music in current theatrical feature films?

I think the rule of the day is a big question mark. The directors and producers should be informed about what to expect out of music. They really don't know. Directors that have been around 10 or 20 years make pictures the best way they know how, and when they get into the cutting room and scoring stage...they become self-conscious. At that point many of them want to be avant-garde. They don't want to get involved with the types of things Franz Waxman used to do so beautifully—he really sang and opened up the screen. I'll always be in love with that school.

What is your feeling with regard to music in feature films made for television?

I think it's difficult to be as subtle with a lot of television as you are with movies because you have a captive audience in movie houses—even these three-hour movie extravaganzas. In television you compete with a can of beer so you have to grab. There is much more music in television than motion pictures. It's loaded with music. They don't have the time for quality control or the time to really dig into the kind of status they want. They set a 10-day schedule, man, and that's it in television. The composer gets the same kind of short time to write the music. I think its a medium unlike films, where you have time to polish. It's a very rough schedule. Many times you are dealing with overall attitudes and you have to jump in and make your kill fast because you don't have time to develop subtle points over a long period.

Do you think that there should be a closer association between the producer and the composer?

Oh my God yes! Not so much the producer. I don't get too hot with the producer for the most part—I think it's the director. For the most part the producer doesn't know what's going on, he's really foggy. He raises the money and has to see that Goldie Hawn's hairdresser flies in from somewhere. The good ones are supposed to stand behind the director—like Bob Whiteman behind Sidney Lumet.

Then your association in films is mostly with the director?

Especially in feature films. It's a very personal relationship. It's his baby. He's been thinking about this thing. He's saying, "I do or do not like this script, I don't like that lighting, I don't like that shot." He's making decisions and molding everything together. I think that he is the only one who has the right to say, "I don't like the harpsichord sound" or whatever. I think it's still part of his sculpture at that point. A producer is usually there to take care of business and mechanical arrangements to backstop the director's taste.

Do you feel that if the average director has had a certain amount of music training, it would be beneficial?

Yes! Sidney Lumet has studied. He can play Bach—all of Bach's things. Somehow that well is a little bit more refined. He knows how to get down to specifics. Otherwise you have to deal in trying to describe *dramatic* broadstrokes on *his* side and *musical* broadstrokes on *my* side. You can't get down to the new answers if they haven't had a music background.

In many of the current spy-type television series there is a use of the so-called big-band jazz style. Do you approve of this?

I don't know. I think that's another kind of psychological thing. I guess it depends on whose hand it's in—the taste. Mancini did a marvelous job out of things that before in television sounded kind of cheap. Every time you'd go to that roadside bar with Brando on the motorcycle with his black jacket and Mamie Van Dorn with her tights on, here's this big band blasting out source music. It had a cheap quality about it. I used to cringe. But Mancini boiled it down to bass flutes, walking basses, and stark things. I think that they should take their call from the *character* of the show and somehow form some unique kind of quality to fit this character.

Do you have the feeling that some composers approach the background score from the standpoint of self-gratification and thus ignore the audience reaction?

No. I couldn't say that honestly. I think basically they try to involve themselves in the act of underscoring a piece of film. They really do. It also depends on the degree of experience. I know the people that understand the craft. I don't think that they would ever violate it in the face of anything for their own self-gratification by disregarding dialog or whatever. If a guy does it out of ignorance, he doesn't know any better. That's different. I don't think you could ever revert back to ignoring the principles once you've gone through the trouble of learning them. The guys I've met are really beautiful conscientious people.

What would be your advice to young producers and directors as to their better understanding of the contribution of music to films?

Most film composers, if they're experienced and have been around, have broad minds, not hung up on just one kind of bag—[and they] have an obligation to be aware and involved in all kinds of music. Usually, the composer has the edge on the producer or director in that he can remember more of a repertoire—a catalog in his mind of different things he can apply and several kinds of approaches inside each category. From the beginning, he has much more to refer to in terms of listening experience. The way the producer or director can catch up to this is to be aware of digging inside the different categories and understanding what the various broadstroke aspects of classical music are all about as well as inside the categories of the pop scene. If a producer or director says today, "I would like a rock group concept for a picture," I wouldn't know what the hell he meant because [of sheer diversity of numbers]—there has to be seven thousand groups out there. They all have different sounds, different musical standards, and [a quality range of] very poor to excellent. You can't say "a rock score." That's too far out—too general—because when you hear "Blood Sweat and Tears" doing Satie there's a lot of idiot groups who think that's some sort of salad dressing. You have to be specific, saying you want to deal with a guitar group, acoustic or electric, because that range goes from Simon & Garfunkel "acoustic" to the San Francisco Haight-Ashbury "acid" sound. There is a vast dramatic difference *with* horns or *without* horns. Is it the *blues* horn group or the *modern* horn group? [There are] so many inside things you have to understand. I would imagine that the best way to really prepare is to listen to a lot of music. It's the only thing you *can* do. Listen to what's going on. An interesting thing about the record business, where I came from, is that it is probably the best barometer to know what people are aware of and how much they can take. [This is] in contrast to the film business, where they can make a two-million-dollar "turkey" and get their two million back with maybe three of four more by just the right kind of merchandising. In the record business you have to make a record that is so close to the pulse of the people that you hear it on the radio free. That's as much as can be done for it. So you hear it, and if you like it you go downtown and buy it.

HUGO FRIEDHOFER

Hugo Friedhofer began his film career in 1929 at Fox Film Studios. Prior to this, he was a cellist and arranger in a motion picture theatre in San Francisco. Following his contract at Fox Studios he worked as an orchestrator for Eric Korngold and Max Steiner at Warner Brothers Studios. Of his many film scores, including *Boy on a Dolphin*, *An Affair to Remember*, *One-Eyed Jacks*, and *The Barbarian and the Geisha*, was the outstanding Academy Award winner, *The Best Years of Our Lives*, which continues to be one of the more important music contributions to the cinema.

May we have your comments on film music patterns, styles, and types?

Well, this is where a big hassle sometimes occurs between the director or producer and the composer, who may visualize an entirely different kind of—I hate to use the word—*background* score. Music, for the most part, is an adjunct, the gravy on the roast beef, that sometimes isn't there. That is where the composer is called upon to do his utmost in the way of persuasion. Of course, if he thinks that the producer is correct in his idea about a musical approach, he has no problem—he will go along with that. In any case, music is the most difficult thing to talk about in any other terms except those of sound. A producer can say to you, "I want something impressionistic" or "I want something nebulous." Well, that can mean a lot of different things. The composer's idea of what is nebulous and impressionistic—which is a loaded word—can be poles apart from what the producer has in mind. The producer is probably thinking of Debussy or he may be thinking of Ravel who, incidentally, is the most classic and unimpressionistic of any of the composers of his generation, in contrary distinction to Debussy. The composer, on the other hand, may have something else in mind, like the current Polish trend in music, or the music of the Viennese—not so much in the style of Anton Webern but more like Alban Berg or Schoenberg, both of which to a certain extent are extremely impressionistic or expressionistic. So right away you have these things and the great difficulty in communication consists in the fact that the composer's concept, which is orchestral of course, is not easily translatable into terms that are playable on the piano by ten fingers. Tone color is also eliminated in a demonstration of this kind. So, unless you are sitting down at the piano and are just playing what we must call—for want of a better word—a tune or a melody, you're dead. You can strike a chord, either simple or complex, on the piano and you can say "now here I hear brass,"—but that chord, without any description at all, can be brass, or woodwind, or strings, or it can be a setup of percussion instruments or electronic instruments. This is where an awful lot of hangups occur.

What are your thoughts about composing to dramatic action, atmosphere, functional music?

I have gotten into a bag where I am more and more opposed to what goes on musically in a score. It's nothing more or less than a duplication of what is occurring visually. You know the old idea—the horse runs: the music runs. It is related to the Mickey Mouse technique, and it is perfectly dandy in cartoons, but it's kind of ridiculous nowadays—unless it's done very, very subtly in film. The idea of a score the way I look at it is to point out, or make the audience aware of, the things that can neither be photographed nor said—the interior motivation, in other words. If the man runs, why is he running? Not the mere manifestation of speed.

Have you had much difficulty in communicating your ideas to producers?

I have been fortunate in dealing with producers who, for the most part, after a little persuasion, were willing to take my word for it. I explained to them that I was a lousy pianist. I could demonstrate a tune or something like that, but when it came to demonstrating what I was writing for a chase, or to fall into that horrible category of *mood* music—which you base not so much on melodic line but on color appropriate to the scene—Iwas lost. And besides I always clinch the argument by saying that I cannot do with 10 fingers what an orchestra of 40 or 50 or even 20 men can do. On the other hand, I have had occasions when producers have come to me and said, "Now you know we can't make up our minds [whether] to use you or so-and-so." Well, in some cases this would be understandable. In other cases the so-and-so would be a composer who worked in a style so completely disparate from mine that I could never understand how they finally decided upon me. Another thing—this may sound a little arrogant, and it's intended to—is the fact that I feel that when a producer hires me, he hires me because he believes that I know my business. And if, after hiring me, he proceeds to try to tell me my business, I have the feeling that he has got hold of the wrong man.

I had great affection for a man about whom there was much controversy as a producer. His name was Jerry Wald. The beautiful part about working for Jerry was that he let you severely alone. Or if he'd ask you a question and you'd give him an answer, he would say "I don't know what you're talking about, but you know your business and I'm sure you are right."

I've made mistakes and have been able to correct them, fortunately. A producer, while a score was in the process of being recorded, would suddenly pick on one isolated sequence and say, "You know, I don't think that you were quite right in this instance. Have you time to try a new approach to it? Well, that's fine and I'm perfectly willing to play along. As Virgil Thompson said, that's the beauty of working with a live composer rather than a dead one. With a live composer you can always have him change his music."

Do you feel that there is an overuse of, shall we say, exotic instruments like electronics and percussion and if so, do you feel that these are used for sensationalism?

Well, there's nothing wrong with a little sensationalism in the right place. I have always been a percussion freak, as a matter of fact—not necessarily percussion from the standpoint of noise, or establishing a rhythm, but rather from the standpoint of an interesting orchestral color. I think that my knowledge of percussion became largely solidified at the time when I was working with Earle Hagen on the *I Spy* series, which was largely done in various locations, like Hong Kong, various parts of Japan, Mexico, North Africa, Greece, and Spain. We had a thing going where we were trying to do a fusion of ethnic music and a certain jazz-oriented approach which was necessary because, as you recall, the two principal characters were rather hip. We felt that it was right rather than go for the straight kind of cloak-and-dagger score. We utilized a great many percussion instruments out of Emil Richards' collection, who was one of our two regular percussionists (we always used two). And there were occasions...when we would use as many as five or even six. I believe, on one occasion, we used a whole battery of drummers.

What are your thoughts regarding the scoring of feature films made for TV?

It's a little hard to tell. I've done one which posed no particular problem. It was sort of a comedy western—not too good, come to think of it, but somehow it managed to sweep everything else off the board the night it was shown: *The Over-the-Hill Gang*. It was about a group of broken-down Texas rangers who were coming to the rescue of a young associate who was trying to clean up a western town under the control of a "baddy." It was fun to do and posed no particular problem. I approached it in exactly the same way that I would a feature theatrical film. As a matter of fact, even in our *I Spy* shows, both Hagen and I had the feeling that except for the length of the music, the approach should not be different from that which we would use in a theatrical film.

What is your opinion in the use of the "Stan Kenton" type of scoring for chase and fight sequences in TV films?

I think there are times when it can be very effective, in that you can by means of it avoid the Mickey Mouse approach of having every blow or kick or fall to the floor pointed up musically. This can get pretty tiresome. In seeing a recent rerun of *Of Mice and Men*, with Copland's score, I noted there was a synchronization between a punch in the mouth and a musical impact, where one canceled the other. Of course one can, in a climactic moment, go in for this kind of synchronization when one of the two combating parties finally dies or is shot or stabbed or something. That's fine; you put a period on the whole thing. However, to point up everything becomes oversynchronous.

What is your opinion of rock-type scoring for films? Do you think this is a passing fad or a trend?

It happens to be stylish right now but it's stylish for no valid reasons. In feature films particularly, it is owing to an unfortunate thing that can be compared to the military— industrial complex that the publishers and recording companies seem to be totally indifferent to the dramatic values of the score. All they're interested in is if this music is going to sell any albums. And I have the feeling that in a great many cases the album was thought of first, and the tracks were turned over to a music editor who simply introduced them into the film where he or the producer thought they were suitable.

Are you aware of Alex North's being very upset in his association with *2001—A Space Odyssey*?

Alex wrote a splendid score for that and then they used a compiled score. Strangely enough, it gave the music of Richard Strauss a new lease on life. All of a sudden people were out buying Strauss symphonic poems. A similar situation arose a great many years ago in connection with a film I orchestrated for Max Steiner at Warner Brothers. It was a picture dealing with a concert pianist, played by Mary Astor, who was supposed to be playing the Tchaikovsky piano concerto in a concert. Well, the release of the film boosted the sales of the concerto like you wouldn't believe. It was just about the time that Freddie Martin did *Tonight We Love*, which also might have been a result of the film.

A common complaint of many composers is that there is too much music used in many films. What do you feel about this?

We went through a period in the thirties and forties when pictures demanded a lot of music. Think of the big costume epics that were turned out at Warner Brothers, films that Steiner and Korngold did. They could stand a lot of music, but it didn't necessarily follow that every picture needed that much. I think the value of silence is very, very important. I have the feeling too, that there has to be some way, which we haven't solved successfully yet, of devising a kind of connective tissue, musically, between places that really do need music strongly, and places that don't. And if you left music out of those places you would immediately have a very spotty kind of score. This happens largely with television because you get 20- or 30-second bridges and cues. If you get 30 seconds you're lucky.

Do you think that there is a misuse, or overuse of the big theme.

That is another one of those things in which an identifying theme sometimes helps the picture but it also helps the sale of records. There are some pictures that do not demand it. There are certain pictures that can be athematic—using no theme at all—music that is literally nothing more than a musically devised sound effect. Other pictures call for a [so-called] "love" theme, and because it's always the same kind of love, it's always the same kind of love theme.

Who do you think is responsible for the desire to have a hit song, or theme, in a film—the composer or the director?

They both would like it, of course. In this connection an anecdote comes to mind which might be amusing. The late Jerome Kern, who needs no particular recommendation from me, was once approached by a producer for whom he was going to do a musical. The producer said to Jerry, "I want you to guarantee me a hit." And Jerry—he always carried his head a little to one side; he looked like an angry molting owl—looked at the producer and said, "If I could guarantee you a hit, I wouldn't be a composer—I'd be a publisher." And with that, he walked away.

DAVID GRUSIN

David Grusin is one of the newer arrivals on the Hollywood scene. He has written themes and functional music scores for *The Name of the Game*, *It Takes a Thief*, *The Ghost and Mrs. Muir*, *Dan August*, *Funny Face*, and others.

Do you feel that there may be certain faults in the creating and application of music to some feature films? If so, what would your suggestion be to correct them?

I think the biggest fault with American pictures is that we tend to load the pictures with too much music. When I say we, I don't necessarily mean only composers, but producers and directors as well. Also, there is some misconception of what music does for pictures. I think the effect of music is determined by the amount in isolated cases. Nevertheless, I think that the trend is getting better. There is more judicious spotting of music and using it really as a function to help the overall feeling of the story. I think the worst fault, particularly in television, is where we seem to be afraid to let anything at all happen. If there is no dialog or if there is a transition to another scene that takes longer than five or ten seconds, we had better load it with music.

Do you feel that there is a lack of communication between many composers and producers and directors?

Yes, of course. Absolutely.

In your opinion how can this be corrected?

I'm not sure it can. When two composers get together it sometimes is not easy to communicate about music even though they both know what the other's talking about. It's even harder when there is no technical understanding on the part of the producer or director. I think the problem lies not only with them. I hate to look at it as if we were on opposite sides. I think it's a mutual problem. We have to be aware of what our function is as composers, as screen composers—just as *they* have to be aware of beautiful cinematography, marvelous optical effects, and so forth. What the director achieves doesn't really mean anything unless he is communicating to an audience. And we're in the same boat; I think that if we don't lose sight of that fact it's much easier to understand what they are saying. That doesn't help them to understand what we're doing necessarily, but if everybody is going in the same direction, it's much easier.

Do you approve of the use of so-called big-band jazz in many of our television spy shows, particularly in connection with chases and fights?

Well I approve of it on a very limited level. It's better than a lot of diminished chords and tremolos. It seems that if you have a chase in a spy show it's like a laid-out pattern that we're supposed to go at automatically. I don't like that aspect at all.

Referring to the many new percussion and electronic instruments, do you feel that they are being used excessively?

They run in cycles it seems. I remember when the synthesizer was first made available out here. Paul Beaver got the franchise and everybody ran down there and found out the basic facts of life about it and that was going to be the solution to all our problems of scoring. [Then] there was a year it became very hip *not* to use it. I think the synthesizer has settled into just one of many music elements to use and I think it's being used judiciously now more than at the outset.

I very much like ethnic instruments. I love the kind of projects that allow you to get into them. Emil Richards is a great collector of mostly Asiatic and Eastern European and African percussion instruments. I love to go to his house and select a few things we are going to use. It's marvelous. Maybe this is digressing from your question, but there is something very sympathetic between a mating of electronically produced sound and film. I don't know why it is. I guess they're both synthetic media. But something seems to work with well recorded and well written electronic music. Maybe it wouldn't hold up if you didn't have the film, but it really seems to be good scoring.

Is the use of electronic instruments caused by a desire for sensationalism?

No. I think good composers, in order to stay alive and interesting and vital, are looking all the time for new devices. If you want to call them gimmicks, they are gimmicks, but it's a way to communicate without using the old technique again—without using sounds that have been used before. I don't think it's sensationalism so much as keeping it interesting and fun to go to work.

What is your opinion of the use of rock groups in scoring many feature films?

I worked on *The Graduate*, and it made a lot of money for the producers. We ended up using Paul Simon's records because we couldn't reproduce that Simon & Garfunkel sound. It's very difficult to reproduce something that you spend a lot of time in a phonograph recording studio trying to get. The point I am trying to make is that the picture did an enormous box office and the songs worked very well in the picture. They weren't really rock songs; they were a little more lyrical—but they "worked." The director cut his picture to them. I have seen this in commercials and feature films, and occasionally in television. Where scenes are cut to music that's already in existence, the music is already a fact. A director chooses to cut his film to the music and it works marvelously; there's something to that. The sound comes first. I don't know what happens, what the chemistry is, but those things really work. Now, other directors and producers in the studios, seeing the success of *The Graduate*, attributed part of the success to the music. Therefore, if they're going to make X millions of dollars on their pictures, they're going to have to get a rock group or a well known popular group, and that's how it's going to work. I think they're still trying it occasionally. However, sometimes it works and sometimes it doesn't. I'm thinking of the picture *Goodbye Columbus*, in which they needed underscoring besides songs.

Do you feel that the excessive uses of the Big Theme are predicated on the possibility of large phonograph record sales, and if so, is this not defeating the purpose of film music, which is to enhance the plot motivation?

Generally, that's true. The overuse of the so-called *big themes* is based on selling records. It is also based on selling the picture. It's also a kind of an old-fashioned way of scoring. Remember some Alfred Newman scores, in which there was really one theme and it was used constantly—that was about the only music, with different orchestration. I'll never believe it's a good idea to have theme music in there just because it's the theme of the picture. It can never be a stronger effect than a correct way of scoring a scene. It will never replace that.

Referring to this big theme, do you feel that excessive uses of these devices is a type of audience brainwash much like TV spot commercials?

Absolutely! And that sometimes definitely comes from the producer or the director. I mean they insist on it. I think it was *Lawrence of Arabia*—David Lean. I think he insisted that the key never be changed—not only the same music, but the same arrangement in the same key.

What would your suggestion be to young producer/directors for improvement of the music contribution to the film, both theatrical and television?

It seems that young producers and directors are much easier to work with in terms of their open-mindedness. I think the best thing is to try to avoid the traps. If they could avoid the trap that a lot of older, very experienced directors and producers fall into, which is if you have a picture about X, try not to expect a score that's going to resemble a score that you can remember from another picture that might have been about X. In other words, try not to think in terms of stereotypes.

I know they're avoiding that as young directors. I feel that most of them are. They're trying to do something new and they should keep in mind that the music seems to help the picture most if you don't try to lay in specific *cliche* kinds of sounds. You shouldn't expect that, even though they may cry for it, even if you are dealing with a western. Westerns can take all kinds of music; they can take twelve-tone music beautifully.

What has been your experience or frustrations regarding the time allotted to create music for television?

There is never enough time; however, I've a particular set of problems in terms of writing. Every time I write, it feels to me like the first time. I don't seem to be able to retain any facility from having written last week. It's like I sit down to a blank page again. I find I need to develop some contempt—either for whoever is making me do this in a very short time or for the show itself. If it presents any problems in order to write quickly, I have to define my hatred of it a little and then get rid of it.

Could you explain the relatively new recording techniques, such as various filtered gimmicks and delayed tracks—things that you might have used or might use?

The biggest frustration I have found as a film composer, is [that] the techniques we use in recording the music are antiquated. They're not bad, the fidelity is very good, etc., but the fact is we are still working with the same equipment. Every new studio that is being built, I'm quite sure, will be installing 16-track tape, maybe 24, with a sync pulse and a way to play back a picture with whatever that machine is. It's fantastic. I mean, you can really do the same things you do in a phonograph record studio. The same techniques. The sounds. I can't tell you what a better sound it would be if you could isolate the rhythm section or keep them from leaking into the strings and thus allow you to bring in the strings with equalization in filters and so forth. New control boards have that whereas the old ones don't. It really depends on what company you are recording for, or if you have a choice of studios. Then you would probably pick the one that had the newer phonograph-recording equipment.

What percentage of producers or directors are in contact with you while you are constructing a score?

Not very many. I suspect mostly because they're into new projects by the time I get into their postproduction. It's okay, too. I have to say it's nice—I like a lot of communication at the beginning and a kind of a direction so that we know where we are going. Then it's nice not to have them. I really hate to audition like "when can I hear the tune?" They can hear the tune when they come on the stage.

Have any producers or directors suggested or demanded changes in your music during recording sessions?

Not many. Maybe 20%. There are seldom major changes. I've never had a disaster—one of those things where they toss the score out. Mostly, I find, if there *is* a question, we go ahead and record. Most of the questions are whether to score the scene or not, and that's no problem because we can take it out during dubbing if they don't want to use it. I've been fairly fortunate.

Do you conduct your own music?

Yes.

What are your feelings about the psychological approach to film music?

That's probably one of the most important aspects of scoring. I think that involves your first attitudes toward specific projects, and it also has to do with your whole attitude toward the medium. To have a controlled kind of contempt for what you do. There's nothing to replace the first time you performed your own music or had somebody else hear it or somebody else play it. And there are extensions of that all the way up and down the line to not only *how is a* producer/director going to accept what I write? or how is an audience going to accept what I am going to write? but how do the players feel about it? because if they hate it, it's not going to be as good as if they love it. Then you start thinking, who am I writing for? You just have to find out who you are with respect to all of these questions. At some point you have to forget about the fact that they are letting me score their picture, and you have to start thinking I am consenting to score their picture for them. Otherwise, you aren't going to write note one; it's never going to get on the paper.

JOHN GREEN

Composer, conductor, arranger, pianist, and producer, John Green is probably one of the most versatile and active musicians to be associated with the film industry. From his beginning as a composer of at least a half-dozen all-time hit songs, including *Coquette, Out of Nowhere, I Cover the Waterfront*, and *Body and Soul*, to the present, in which his activities are largely as a symphony conductor, his career has been marked with much success. General music director for **MGM Studios** for 10 years, Green has received 14 Oscar nominations plus five Academy Awards (*Easter Parade, An American in Paris, Westside Story*, and *Oliver*).

Mr. Green, do you feel a lack of communication between composers and many producers?

I think that situation is perhaps somewhat better than we knew in the beginning because that catastrophic lack of communication, to which your question refers, was productive of such tensions and such inefficiencies and such failure to realize the total potential of music in relation to films, it was inevitable that the situation would improve somewhat. But there's still a great deal of room for further improvement.

What would your suggestion be to improve this situation?

Well, I think the first thing, and this may offend some of our musical tyros, is on the composer's side. Now you and I know so well that we all feel that the composer should be on the picture from the time that the screen writer is on it. And that the screenplay with which the musical element will eventually be amalgamated should be conceived in terms of what all the elements, including music, are going to be. And, therefore, the composer should be there when the guy with the typewriter is first there. The music, like the lighting, like the photography, like the costumes, like the design and the scenery, is there for the purpose of implementing the impact of the dramaturgy of the piece. That's what it's for. Therefore, it is corollary, and the composer has to realize that it's the producer's and the director's picture. It's not the composer's picture. That doesn't mean that the composer has to be a servant and carry the musical tray in to the table that he is told to put it on; that's not what I'm getting at. But the composer has to realize, as does the actor, that it's his number one function to implement the dramatic action.

What is your opinion of music in feature films made for TV, generally speaking?

I cannot think of any stereotype that surpasses the stereotypism of much of TV music today. I can't listen to most of it anymore. Of course, there are great exceptions. In the first place, there is so much of varying degrees of blood and thunder, tragedy or tension on television, how many musical devices can there be? You spin the dial, you go from one channel to another, the scores are practically interchangeable. We are living at a time of the so-called *new wave*. We are living in an atmosphere of young people. Nobody wants anybody who's been around for more than 10 years. So, I, for one, haven't been doing a lot of television lately—not in some time. I'm damned if I know what I'd do with a *Medical Center*, a *Mission Impossible*, or *Hawaii Five-O*. I don't think I could avoid being stereotyped.

I would like a romantic story or a comedy. Then I might be able to avoid the stereotype. Nevertheless, there *are* some very talented and skillful people writing. Elmer Bernstein, Lalo Shrifrin, Quincy Jones, young Billy Goldenberg, and Leonard Rosenman, to name a few.

What is your opinion of the current jazz type scoring in many of our spy-type TV series programs?

I think so much of this causation is ecological. Ecological, meaning environmental, can be stretched to include the intellectual, esthetic, and artistic environment as well as the physical environment. The need for hyperbolic stimulation, which is in itself enervating and destructive, characterizes our times. People laugh too loud. They talk too loud. They laugh too much, and they talk too much. Everything is too much. This is one of the all-pervading sicknesses of our time. Even in terms of the human physique, we have a situation of epidemic hearing loss at this point. I don't know whether you are personally acquainted with Dr. Victor Goodhill, who is perhaps the world's leading authority on the mechanics, psychology, anatomy and physiology of the ear in relation to the nervous system and the brain. Only two weeks ago I had the privilege of having a long listen to Victor Goodhill. He was telling me about the researches of his institute into the damage to the human hearing mechanism caused by not only sheer volume, but by the incessant impact of percussive sounds on the ear. Nevertheless, like dope, which is terribly destructive, this is needed by the sound addict as dope is needed by the dope addict. I think that this has more to do with the incidence of the kind of music that you are talking about than any really dramatically valid reasons.

What would be your suggestions to young producers in order to attempt to improve film music in the future?

I think the first thing they should do is study films like *The Informer*, with that incredibly wonderful score of Max Steiner; *All That Money Can Buy* by Bernard Herrmann; *Jane Eyre*, also by Herrmann; *Objective Burma* by Franz Waxman; *The Cobweb* by Leonard Rosenman. I mention *Cobweb* because it's so contrasting to the Max Steiner school. *Cobweb* was the first organized twelve-tone score written for pictures that I know of. Then, of course, Alfred Newman's score for *Wuthering Heights*. Pictures of that nature. Study those scores, which by anyone's standards fulfill their dramatic obligations to the nth degree. Having studied them, the young and potentially great producer then perhaps decides that he doesn't see, stylistically, that sound for the picture that he is making. A totally different sound is needed. But by studying those great scores, the young producer will have been exposed to the wonders of what music can do dramatically. Now I am going to surprise you by naming another picture that any young producer should study from the point of view of what to do about music: *Midnight Cowboy*. Now that was a compiled job, in the charge of John Barry. It was a score that used previously made recordings and all kinds of electronic sounds and effects. This is a totally different kind of score from any of the other that I have mentioned, which are in the conventional mode to one degree or another. But John Barry's score of *Midnight Cowboy* looked rather more forward as a textbook of what's right for a film. I envied John for having done that job. (I wonder if I would have known where to begin.) Any young producer should study that score.

Elmer Bernstein's *To Kill a Mockingbird* was a brilliant score, dramatically. The next thing a young producer should do is to go to some concerts, and at least by osmosis get some acquaintance with the materials of music and the makings thereof. Then a young producer should attend a recording session of an Elmer Bernstein, Jerry Goldsmith, Lenny Rosenman, to see how the master technicians work. And try to understand the composer's problems, and develop some kind of current touch with both the technology and the esthetics. I mean, a producer who is worthy of the name can talk to his designer at least in a communicative language. One of the big problems between composers and producers has been the failure to find any kind of a common language. Composers and producers, in order to be effective in implementing their work together, have to be able to communicate. The basic language of a producer is not the basic language of a composer, and vice versa. They must each learn enough of the other fellow's basic language to be able to have not necessarily a "yessing" arrangement, but an arrangement that permits a viable colloquy. That's vitally important.

With so many old feature films being shown on TV, do you feel that the new young audience could be confused between the older music approach and the present-day, more progressive approach?

I think "confused" is an unfortunate word. I think they will be stimulated to question, which I think is healthy. I feel that effective exposure to the best of the past is essential to the ability to build an effective present.

In the case of the big theme such as employed in *Dr. Zhivago* and *Love Story*, do you have the feeling that this device is overdone in many film scores?

When you talk about *Zhivago*, you talk about *THE* example. I thought if I'd heard that theme once more in

Zhivago, I would need medical treatment. But go fight 2½ million copies of the album!

Again referring to the big theme, is it possible that this may be an audience brainwash like spot commercial jingles?

Yes. Its essential origin really was the leitmotif technique of Wagner. So that's a big topic. As a matter of fact, I devote a whole lecture to the practicality and limitations of the use of leitmotif technique. Yes, I think it's very useful when tastefully, knowledgeably, and brilliantly handled. I'm not a Hollywood panner; I love Hollywood; I hate to hear it panned mercilessly and gratuitously. But we are a community of excesses. I think that's the trouble. We latch onto something, and it's like having a beautiful, georgeous lemon, then juicing it on an electric juicer, and then trying to get more juice by stamping the skin underfoot.

ALEX NORTH

Alex North has probably one of the most thorough music backgrounds of any film composer. A graduate of Juillard, he studied composition and orchestration in Moscow for two years; had private instruction with Aaron Copland, Ernst Toch, and Roger Sessions; received piano instruction at the Curtis Institute; composed music for many documentaries, the ballet, the theatre, and the Martha Graham modern dance group.

He has been composing music for films since 1950, the first of which was *A Streetcar Named Desire*. His long list of credits include *Death of a Salesman, Who's Afraid of Virginia Woolf?*, *Spartacus*, and *Cleopatra*.

Do you feel a lack of communication between many composers and producers or directors?

I've been fortunate in having a mutual respect, depending on the producer or the director. For example, Fred Zinneman or John Huston or Elia Kazan would say, "Alex, we appreciate your work and we respect you, so you go ahead and do what you feel is right." On the other hand, I've had miserable experiences with certain directors and producers where, after the score has been written, issue would be taken with certain scenes, and if I'd agree, I would make the change right on the spot. But in several cases, after I was off the scene, music would be taken out without my knowledge, which was very upsetting. I don't think that every note I write is precious and has to be in the score, because I would be the first to say, at the rerecording, that it's not right.

Do you feel that many of the new percussion and electronic instruments are being used extensively?

Perhaps I haven't seen enough films that have used electronics and percussion, but certainly in the few that I have seen, I think that kind of approach has been overextended. And what the producers and directors call the *new sound* is over, too. I think it's time to get back to using what I try to achieve through the legitimate orchestra: a simulated sound of electronics.

Do you approve of the big-band jazz sound in many of our TV spy shows, particularly in connection with chases and fights?

I think that's overdone. I think I was one of the first to use jazz in *Streetcar*, and subsequently in other films. But there is a kind of writing today that seems so repetitious and so without profile, style, individual style, that you expect the bongos here and the timbales there. It's again taking advantage of a period of maybe the early sixties, where this kind of approach was used and used successfully. The whole pattern in filmmaking is to use what has been successful before and what is commercial, so that an album can be extracted from the score and will help promote the film.

What is your opinion of the use of rock groups in scoring many feature films?

I think it rarely makes sense because they're set pieces for the most part, and the right way to score a film is to tailor the music to the particular scene, not that it has to make very many changes during the sequence. I'll never forget witnessing films at the Canadian Film Festival. I was a juror there, and [noted that] 99% of the scores were "rock" types. Bosley Crowther, who was one of the judges, would say, "now we're ready for the bongos" and there they were. Or the guitars. I think it's a mechanical thing, and again, a commercial thing. There are composers who write a three-minute piece for a two-minute sequence, so that it works in the album and then just arbitrarily fade out at the end of the scene.

You mentioned before your distress in writing music and then having the producer discard it. Can you recall a case in point where this happened to you on a large scale?

I had an unfortunate experience. It was my greatest opportunity: to do the music for *2001—A Space Odyssey*. I went to London. Stanley Kubrick (the producer) had called me at the Chelsea Hotel in New York. The producer had been working on this film for close to four years and had been using temporary tracks of Mahler, Khatchaturian, and Strauss. He became so accustomed to hearing these tracks that when I came in with something that I thought was contemporary in sound, he used what I would call a Victorian sound approach to a film that demanded something more progressive. This has happened, of course, with other directors who have used temporary tracks for previews. In the case of *Giant*, for example, Ray Heindorf dug out a temporary score and the director got so accustomed to this, he refused to use the new score.

Do you feel that the excessive use of the big theme, such as in the cases of *Doctor Zhivago* and *Love Story*, is predicated on the possibility of large phonograph-record sales, and if so, is this not defeating the purpose of music in films, that being to enhance the plot motivation?

No question about it. I don't know how many times, even on the film that I am working on now, the request has been for a theme that can be used and reused and repeated so that it can step out as a popular song, and that's what happens. There was a good song in *The Sandpiper*. When I saw the film, I was surprised at tₕe number of times the theme was used, and very often it didn't mean anything in terms of the dramatic conflict at that moment. Since this is more or less a commercial field, the composer is in a lousy spot to have to accommodate the producer or director with a theme. That's the trend today.

You have been credited with many excellent film scores; could you describe your method of approach to any given dramatic film that you have scored?

It depends. When I have done large-scope epic films, like *Spartacus* and *Cleopatra*, in both instances I was fortunate in having at least a year to work on these films, and it gave me enough time to do as much research as possible, for reworking and discarding a lot of material, and using a lot of counterpoint. In *Spartacus* I wrote a temporary track for two pianos and two percussions for the battle scenes, which the editor used as a temporary track to cut the film. I thought this was very intelligent. That's when you're fortunate enough to have time. *Who's Afraid of Virginia Woolf?* was one of the most difficult scores to write because of the dynamic and constant dialog in the film. I think it's much more difficult to write a score for a simple film where there is interpersonal relationships and conflict as opposed to a large-scale sound. My fortunate experience was in writing for all those dancers in New York, and for the theatre, where I was limited to only four instruments. Because of union regulations, I had to extend my craft to write a score for a small combination, which I prefer. I prefer chamber orchestras any time. I don't like the idea of cushioning a scene with nondescript music that's there and isn't there. I believe film music is like an approach to opera; one should be aware of it.

I have always debunked the idea that if you're aware of it, it's wrong. I think one *should* be aware of it; if the music is wrong, it's obtrusive.

The common complaint of most composers is that there is too much music in the majority of films. Do you agree?

It depends again on the director and producer. Some feel that they have the music and if the scene doesn't come off right, they've got the music to help the scene. Music can very rarely go above or beyond the scene itself. In approaching the film, my personal way of doing it is to write several ideas and then remold them in accordance with a scene in terms of developing certain [elements of] tension and relaxation. And by doing it logically, it's possible that the music itself will have a beginning, a middle, and an end. For one thing, I think most films are overscored. I think it's a question of the taste of the director and composer to decide what particular scenes demand or need music to implement, to bring another dimension—just as lighting or costuming or whatever—to the film.

What would be your suggestion to producers and directors for improvement of the music contribution to films, both theatrical and television?

Well, first of all, they have to have experience in seeing enough films to judge what approach is most suitable for a particular story or what I call the key to the score. I think they should have as much contact with a composer as possible and get him in early in making the film if it's financially possible. Of course, we know the reason why we are brought in at the end of the film. It's because we're given a certain number of weeks to write the score and if it's over a certain length of time, then they have to pay us *pro rata*. I think the ideal thing is to give the composer the book, a scenario, or a script to read, and to sit with the producer and discuss the approach musically, if he is musically inclined. I always appreciate it, even as awkward as a producer or director may be in stating what he wants in music, and I will jot down a word or two of what he says, so that I get a feeling of what they're seeking musically.

Do you think if they had a basic music education it would help?

No question about it. They should be exposed to music that's been written for opera, for ballet. Stravinski's written any number of pieces of functional music, as we do for films, that work for its particular purpose at the time, even though it may be sectional. The young producer or director should be aware of the various approaches to functional music. I've devoted so much of my life to writing for ballet, despite the fact that I've done so-called absolute music as well. This is much more difficult because when you have a film you have a cue sheet (which is a crutch) and you know where you are going musically. However, you still face a blank sheet of music every morning, whether it's for a film or a string quartet.

The effects of film music on the audience—would you have anything to comment about that?

I don't think the audience is that aware of the contribution of music. I think it's great, now and then, to get a fan letter from someone out in the hinterlands or some other country who writes you a letter or makes a comment about certain scenes or a certain kind of scoring. I still feel that generally and culturally, the American audience isn't educated enough, or aware enough, of the contribution of music and what it can do for a film. That's one of the advantages of going out to universities and colleges and getting the stimulus of questions from youngsters who are very much more aware of what music is about for films.

ARTHUR MORTON

Arthur Morton, composer, conductor, orchestrator, and arranger has been associated with film music for some 40 years. He has composed scores for many films and TV series. He was associated for five years with the TV series *Peyton Place* as composer and conductor. At present he is composer—conductor for *The Waltons.*

During his career, he has orchestrated for many of the foremost Hollywood composers, including Jerry Goldsmith, Alex North, Hugo Friedhofer, and George Duning.

Mr. Morton's diversified activities have given him a completely objective view of not only composing but filmmaking in general.

Is the director the person who is now making decisions regarding music, whereas some time ago the producer was in charge?

That's correct. Today the director is the big man, particularly with the wave of younger people. When my son was at Harvard, for example, there was a group of film buffs who considered the most important man in the film, if it wasn't Humphrey Bogart, was the director.

As we know, there existed contracts between the producers and the directors in which the director was allowed to view only the final cut after which he no longer participated in the postproduction contribution. What ever happened to this?

In many areas that still works. It brings to mind a Blake Edwards film that I worked on with Jerry Goldsmith at MGM. It was called *The Wild Rovers.* Now Blake Edwards is a pretty big name, and [he is] a very capable man. After the film was finished, it probably needed a little judicious cutting because the preview was not too good. After Edwards had made the first cut Jim Aubrey, the head of MGM at that time, took the film away from him and just cut the whole picture to ribbons. Therefore, the producer still retains that option.

Even so, are not the producers leaning more and more on the directors?

Yes. But in this particular instance, it's an attitude that I argue with. If a director makes a picture, and cuts it, then takes it out to preview and it bombs, or is a huge success, you can turn that film upside down in 20 million ways and ruin it. But, if you leave in the original concept (which must have been valid or they would not have gone ahead with the picture), and do the best you can with it but don't destroy...then if it is released and doesn't make money, it at least might win some critical acclaim. You see, I think a director can be completely ruined by this haphazard front-office slashing of a picture.

As I mentioned before, the most important guy, to the young people, is the director. It is as it was in the old days, to a certain extent. If John Huston made a film, he was the boss, for the most part. Also, when William Wyler made a picture, he was the boss. If you work with a creative producer like Samuel Goldwyn, that is one thing. If you work for a guy who is a businessman and a dealmaker, there is no reason for him to have that much say because he is basically a dealmaker. Of course, the big directors are not infallible. Even a man of the caliber of a Bob Weiss will make mistakes. The entertainment business is fraught with risk.

What happens when a director who has a solid music background works with a composer? Is there not a danger of a too-intellectual approach to the music?

In this case they are incompetent people.

Wouldn't you think that this could happen?

Of course, it often happens that people can go off the deep end. The end always to be served is to make a dramatic film work, and to make every element that is in it pay off and contribute to the drama. I've known so many composers that have said, "Look, I've written a nice little fugue here. Isn't that great?" And I have said, "Yes, that's great, but what does it have to do with the picture?" The wonderful thing about the accepted repertoire in music, that we think is so great and has been accepted for so many generations, is the dramatic quality. For example, the Beethoven Septet. That's a whale of a show. You wonder if the horn player is going to make it. A Brahms symphony—this is a big dramatic utterance. To me all great music has the quality of cohesiveness and architecture and showmanship. If it doesn't have showmanship, I don't care what the art form is, it's not going to make it. Take a painting—a Picasso, a Renoir, a Rembrandt. The dramatic quality distinguishes from a hack quality by someone who has something to say. This holds true in all of the arts. The dramatic quality of the old Mexican ruins, the Sistine Chapel, Saint Peter's, the Vatican.

Is not film music greatly controlled by the phonograph record business?

Yes, and it's also in the hands of music writing primitives. In yesterday's trade paper I read something about a film composer whom I did not know. It was regarding his score for a special to be broadcast last night. So I listened to it. In this film the composer, who is a pretty good songwriter in the modern idiom (guitars and sustained fiddles), had a valid song, with lyrics. This song was used at times throughout the film, not ineffectively. But the shocking thing was the music between the songs. I assume that he composed this music because his was the only name on the credits. The left-handedness of it, the primitive quality, the ineptness—it was shocking! There is a great difference between a man who can write a tune and a man who knows how to use it throughout the film.

I think we have to be careful in the generality that a valid tune can be used too much. It is dependent upon what the picture is and the composer's judgment and how much variation he can find. This terrible resolution that the most important thing is to have a hit tune or a hit record or a hit album is garbage. The important thing for years has been to have decent music. Now if you have a *Laura*, an exception, it comes out great, but the important thing is to write the music that fits the film, which Raksin did.

Are the new and unusual music sounds the result of newer recording techniques such as multiple tracks, overlays, delayed reverberation, etc?

A lot of that is old technique. Most of it is the electronic instruments themselves. The electric flute, the electronic clarinet, trumpet. This all helps to create these new unusual sounds if used intelligently. It was used in *Patton* with such imagination by Jerry Goldsmith. He has always been three years ahead of the rest in the use of these electronics. Instead of using these devices as a crutch, however, we should only use them as an addition to the dramatic score. With due respect to these electronic instruments and their versatility and their value, it still doesn't take the place of music. If not used that way, most of it is not productive, not fruitful, because it's in the hands of primitives who are overcome with the paraphernalia rather than having an actual concern for the music per se.

What do you think are the basic faults in the application of music to certain feature films?

The worst thing is that so many composers really know nothing about music and they don't seem to care. If they get a couple of banjos and electronic garbage they think this will be a hit record. However, the percentages are still the same. You can have Quincy Jones do every picture in Hollywood and there will [still] be only a few hit albums—he has his mortality rate just like everyone else.

Do you feel a lack of communication between many composers and producers or directors?

I've always felt a lack of communication between *good* composers and producers or directors. The present batch of primitives is speaking in the same musical language as the producers and directors because they're all "tin-ears." It's always been difficult for a man of real imagination to communicate. I have come across very few directors who are at all aware. The last picture that I did with Jerry Goldsmith, Tom Tryon, producer of the film, was tremendously moved by the material. I think the director was also.

Also, I must say this. Many composers have the quality of charisma in their relationship with producers and directors. Men like Tiomkin and evidently Jarre, could dish out anything and the producer would think it's great. This is a very valuable asset. In other words, rather than studying music, one should study with Tiomkin on how to socialize and mix with producers and directors and get the work.

Index

Index